TRACING YOUR
BELFAST ANCESTORS

FAMILY HISTORY FROM PEN & SWORD BOOKS

TRACING YOUR BELFAST ANCESTORS

A Guide for Family Historians

CHRIS PATON

Pen & Sword
FAMILY HISTORY

First published in Great Britain in 2023 by
PEN AND SWORD FAMILY HISTORY
An imprint of
Pen & Sword Books Ltd
Yorkshire – Philadelphia

ISBN 978 1 52678 033 1

Typeset by Mac Style
Printed and bound in the UK by CPI Group (UK) Ltd,
Croydon, CR0 4YY.

Pen & Sword Books Limited incorporates the imprints of Atlas, Archaeology,
Aviation, Discovery, Family History, Fiction, History, Maritime, Military,
Military Classics, Politics, Select, Transport, True Crime, Air World, Frontline
Publishing, Leo Cooper, Remember When, Seaforth Publishing, The Praetorian
Press, Wharncliffe Local History, Wharncliffe Transport, Wharncliffe True
Crime and White Owl.

For a complete list of Pen & Sword titles please contact

PEN & SWORD BOOKS LIMITED
47 Church Street, Barnsley, South Yorkshire, S70 2AS, England
E-mail: enquiries@pen-and-sword.co.uk
Website: www.pen-and-sword.co.uk

Or

PEN AND SWORD BOOKS
1950 Lawrence Rd, Havertown, PA 19083, USA
E-mail: Uspen-and-sword@casematepublishers.com
Website: www.penandswordbooks.com

CONTENTS

INTRODUCTION

Although I was born in Northern Ireland, I had no sooner said hello to the midwives and nurses at the Moyle Hospital in Larne than I was almost immediately whisked off to reside in Scotland, and then England, for the first eight years of my life. It was not until 1979 that I eventually returned to Northern Ireland, to be raised in Carrickfergus on the shores of Belfast Lough, for the rest of my childhood and early adult years.

Carrickfergus was a small town, with some of the most fascinating history in Ireland (often described as 'the history of Ulster writ small'), but whilst growing up there, if I told somebody that I was 'heading up to town' for a bit, it was not to Carrick that I was referring. On the horizon, just 9 miles along the lough from its harbourside, the twin cranes of Harland and Wolff's shipyards would glint in the sunlight, whilst the hills beyond the Knockagh monument, overlooking the real object of my conversation, receded into a haze. When I 'headed up to town', I was going to Belfast.

It is hard to describe the city of Belfast from my youth without experiencing a variety of deep emotions. As a young teenager, Belfast was my weekend escape from school and family life in Carrick, a twenty-minute train journey to York Road Station, and from there into Royal Avenue and Smithfield market, where I would spend the money earned from my daily paper round on books and comics. It was also the city where my 'posh' golf-mad aunt lived, Sheila Cobby, who resided just off the Antrim Road in the city's Fortwilliam area, just a few minutes' walk away from Belfast Castle. When my family first moved back to Carrick from England, it was Sheila who picked us up from the ferry in Belfast, and who gave us our first meal there at her house. Looking at the steak before him, my younger brother asked me what it was, to which I responded with deadly accuracy that it was 'meat in a lump'. We had only ever eaten minced beef whilst living in Plymouth; Belfast was well posh. Years later, when I married in County Kilkenny in 2000, Sheila popped down from the north and made quite the impact; years later my wife's family is still talking about 'Aunty Sheila from Belfast'!

But Belfast also had a serious image problem, being a deeply troubled city from the 1960s to 1970s, often displaying some of the very best of humanity, and at times, some of the worst. To visitors, of which there were seemingly few, it was a God-fearing, sectarian cityscape of 'themuns' and 'usuns' (them and us), filled with barriers, painted kerb stones and intimidating gable-end murals. A city where security guards would check under bus seats and within people's bags for explosive devices, before permitting entry to its shops and arcades. There were endless bomb alerts, regular terrorist atrocities, and the inevitable bomb-damage sales in the shops.

Yet, paradoxically, Belfast was a city where communities would also help each other out at the drop of a hat, where virtually everyone had the same sense of 'crack' or 'craic', and sardonic humour, even if, at times, they could not share it with each other. Often such humour would manifest itself in graffiti. In the mid-1980s, a loyalist slogan on one wall, stating 'Never forsake the blue skies of Ulster for the grey mist of an Irish republic', was greeted on another by a republican riposte, 'Ulster Says No, but the man from Del Monté says "Yes", and he's an Orange man!' – a play on the Orange Order by referring to a popular orange juice commercial at the time. You may not always have agreed with the 'other side', but at times the wit could be appreciated, even if occasionally a lip had to be bitten in so doing.

As I got older, and as the political situation changed, Belfast further opened itself up to me. From 1989 to 1991, I studied at the University of Ulster's campus in the city for a Higher National Diploma in graphic design, and began to experience life there as a young adult. It had, and still has, some amazing bars and restaurants, great cinemas, and some of the best culture on earth. The chocolate fudge cake at Kelly's Cellars, just off Royal Avenue, was God's gift to the city, beaten only by God's gifts to mankind, the city's pastie baps and its Ulster fries. I later moved to England, in 1991, to continue my studies in Bristol, and to then take up work with the BBC, before moving to Scotland in 1997. When the year 2000 arrived, everything changed once again, as the real interest of my life finally revealed itself – the pursuit of family history.

I had little idea how much of a presence Belfast had within my ancestral make-up until I started to look. I knew that my father had been born there and had briefly lived by the Sandy Row as a child, before

The Belfast campus of Ulster University, previously the University of Ulster.

his parents separated and he moved to Carrick with my grandmother, but that was it. I soon discovered that my paternal grandparents had actually moved to Belfast from Glasgow, Scotland, in the late 1930s, and that was as far back as my connection to the city stretched on their lines.

However, my mother's Graham family had a much longer association with the city. As is the case with so many of our Belfast ancestors, my three times great-grandparents had moved there from rural Ulster, not long after they married in 1840. Thomas Graham was originally from the parish of Tynan in County Armagh, whilst Eliza Taylor was from Tehallan (Tyholland) in Monaghan. For the next three decades, Thomas worked as a reeling master at the mill of the York Street Flax Spinning Company, whilst Eliza raised their family at home in North Belfast. One of their sons, my two times great-grandfather Edwin, a riveter at Harland and Wolff (p.8), later lived at Mountcollyer Street, which he signed as his home address in the Ulster Covenant of 1912 (p.11). If you are unfamiliar with Mountcollyer Street, it is the main setting for Kenneth Branagh's wonderful 2021 film, *Belfast*. In addition to my Graham line, I have Smyths, Wattons, Kanes, Bills, Montgomerys and Taylors in the city, whilst just beyond its modern boundaries other lines such as the Bills, Coulters, Gibbs, and Gordons occasionally ventured in for employment and leisure. I have uncovered many extraordinary ancestral stories about them, using many fascinating resources and repositories.

This book is primarily aimed at those starting to look for their Belfast ancestors for the first time, but I hope it will also be of use to those who have already stuck their toe in the Lagan. As with my previous Pen and Sword books, *Tracing Your Irish Family History on the Internet (2nd edition)* and *Tracing Your Irish Ancestors Through Land Records*, it is my hope once again to prove that despite the desperate burden that Irish genealogy is sometimes labelled with, concerning the survival of records, the glass is most definitely half full and not half empty.

Throughout the book, you will find detailed discussions about various records that can be used for research, with occasional case studies and tips thrown in for good measure, as drawn from years of engaging with collections both offline and online. This seems as good a place as any to give you the first one!

TIP: If a website appears to have died, try to find a stored or 'cached' version of it through the Internet Archive's Wayback Machine at **https://web.archive.org**. PRONI's Web Archive at **www.nidirect. gov.uk/articles/about-proni-web-archive** may further help.

Please note that in a small number of cases, in order to avoid printing lengthy website addresses (URLs) in the main text, I have used the Bitly platform (**https://bitly.com**) to create shortcut addresses. The original URLs for these addresses can be found on page 176.

The author's Belfast-born grandparents, Ernest Graham (1922–1971) and Martha Smyth (1922–2001), as pictured in their 1953 passports.

Once again, a huge thanks to my wife Claire, and sons Calum and Jamie, for their ongoing support, and to all at Pen and Sword who have helped to pull the volume before you together. A big thanks also to various folk back home just over the water – to Stephen Scarth and the staff at PRONI, to Darren Topping at Belfast Central Library, to Ann Robinson at NIFHS, to Belfast City Council and the staff at the City Crematorium, to Dr Jonathan Mattison at the Museum of Orange Heritage, to Daniel Horowitz at MyHeritage, and to the Electoral Office of Northern Ireland. This book is dedicated to a few folk. First to the memory of the Patons from Belfast, especially my father Colin (1945–2021) and my aunt Sheila (1943–2013), and then also to the noble Grahams and Smyths from Edmond Street and Liffey Street, including my mad wee granny, Martha Jane Bill Elisabeth Watton Graham (née Smyth; 1922–2001), whose name alone was a genealogical voyage.

Above all though, this one's for the good folk of Belfast – long may the craic reign!

Chapter 1

A WEE HISTORY OF BELFAST

The City of Belfast today is part of the Belfast Metropolitan Area, holding a population of over 600,000, of whom just under a half live within the main city itself. It is the fifteenth largest city in the UK, and on the island of Ireland the second largest, containing about half the population of Dublin. As with all great urban communities, however, Belfast started from much humbler beginnings.

Béal Feirste

The name Belfast, or *Béal Feirste* in the Irish language (*Gaeilge*), derives from the Irish words *béal*, meaning 'mouth' or 'approach', and *fearsaid*, for 'sandbank', and describes the place where a settlement was formed at a fording area between two tributaries of the River Lagan. These were the River Farset, sealed under the modern High Street and Victoria Street area of the city between 1770 and 1804, and the River Blackstaff, which has been mostly covered over since the late nineteenth century, running west close to Chichester Street and diverting south around the north-western corner of Donegall Square.

As a strategic site, this area offered an important means for controlling the mouth of the Lagan, with a castle erected on the site from as early as the twelfth century, attended by a small village. As a settlement, however, its significance in medieval times was dwarfed in importance by two settlements on either side of the sea lough which approached it. In the early medieval period, the sixth-century abbey at nearby Bangor, County Down, provided a seat of ecclesiastical learning. On the County Antrim side, the town of Carrickfergus (also known as Knockfergus), became the stronghold of Norman-dominated east Ulster from the late twelfth century. The earliest inhabitants lived in the settlement's first parish, Shankill, derived from the Irish *sean chill*, meaning 'old church'.

By the fifteenth century, the power of the Norman earldom in Ulster had declined, and control of the area had shifted to a branch of the powerful O'Neill family through the kingdom of Clandeboye (*clan Aedha buidhe*, 'the family of fair-haired Hugh'). It strengthened the castle at Belfast and built another at Castlereagh, but by the mid-sixteenth century, the English Crown had asserted its power, bringing the local chieftain Hugh O'Neill under its influence, albeit with continuing tensions between the O'Neills and the English.

In the aftermath of the sixteenth century English Reformation, a new policy of private plantations was implemented by the Protestant Tudor queen of England, Elizabeth I, who feared the potential power of Ireland's Roman Catholic chieftains to thwart her ambitions on the island. Through these colonies she encouraged English 'adventurers' to try to pacify the more rebellious parts of the province of Ulster and bring it under the control of her administration in Dublin. Despite attempts to grant lands around Belfast to her loyal subjects, it would not be until the aftermath of the Flight of the Earls in 1607, when Hugh O'Neill, the 2nd Earl of Tyrone, fled from Ireland, that everything changed.

The charter town
In 1599, Sir Arthur Chichester, son of a Devonshire noble, came to Ireland to succeed his brother John in the governorship of Carrickfergus, including the lands around Belfast. As a military commander fighting the forces of the Earl of Tyrone in the Nine Years' War, he earned a fierce reputation. In 1605, Chichester was made Lord Deputy of Ireland by Elizabeth's cousin and successor, James I of Britain, a post he held until 1616, and at a time when a larger plantation scheme of Protestant Scots and English settlers was enacted by the king across most of Ulster's counties. Amongst Chichester's first acts was the removal of the ruins of the old castle in Belfast, to be replaced by a larger brick structure.

Belfast started to host markets and fairs from 1605, but on 27 April 1613, a Crown charter was granted to the town to become a corporation. Under the terms of this document, the new borough corporation could manage the town's economy and affairs through a body comprising twelve burgesses, with an annually elected 'sovereign' or mayor, with John Vesey the first to take office, along with the lord of the castle and his deputy. Workers could settle in the town as freemen if they had property or had completed an apprenticeship there. As one of forty new such charter towns in Ireland, the corporation had the right to send two elected burgesses to the Dublin parliament to represent it, with the first being Sir John Blennerhasset, Baron of the Exchequer, and George Trevallian, Esq.

TIP: A useful resource describing life in the borough over its first two centuries of existence, is *The Town Book of the Corporation of Belfast 1613–1816*. This was compiled in 1892 by Robert M. Young from the original town book manuscripts, and reprinted in 2008. The book details many of the day-to-day orders and bye-laws enacted in the early town, as well as naming the town's most prominent inhabitants, with rolls naming freemen, sovereigns and burgesses, when they were appointed, and any dues paid.

In practice, the corporation's powers were limited, with control staying firmly within Chichester's hands. After his death in 1625, his title of Baron Chichester of Belfast was conveyed to his brother Edward, and then from 1647 to Edward's son Arthur as the 1st Earl of Donegall. Subsequent holders of the earldom continued to retain influence over the city's affairs until the nineteenth century.

Belfast was spared the fate of much of Ireland's Protestant settlers in the 1641 Irish rebellion, but in 1644, during the Wars of the Three Kingdoms, it was briefly seized by a Scottish Covenanting army, under General Monroe. Although Scottish settlers in the Plantations of Ulster had been largely Presbyterian, the infrastructure in the province was very firmly designed with the Church of Ireland (the 'Anglican' or 'Episcopalian' church from England) calling the ecclesiastical shots. When the Scottish army arrived, they formally established Presbyterian structures for governance, with the first 'presbytery' created in nearby Carrickfergus. It would not be until 1648 that the town was relieved by English parliamentary forces, but Presbyterianism was by now embedded.

With the Restoration of Charles II in 1660, Belfast's population and influence continued to grow, with a continued mass influx of Scottish Presbyterians. Soon it was outperforming its neighbour at Carrickfergus, trading heavily with overseas clients. An account from the mid-1680s describes Belfast as 'furnished with houses, little orchards, and gardens, besides a very fine park, belonging to the Donegall family, well stored with venison'. At the start of the 'Glorious Revolution' in 1689, the town's charter was briefly revised under the authority of James II to expand the number of burgesses to thirty-five, eighteen of them Roman Catholic gentry, before being restored to its original composition by the Williamite army under the Duke of Schomberg. On 14 June 1690, William III arrived in the town, staying for five nights, before venturing on to his destiny at the Boyne, to battle his predecessor.

By the end of the century, the town's burgesses and merchants had become wealthy property owners, with many departing their Presbyterian faith and converting to the Church of Ireland, to secure their new social status. In 1704, the first Bible printed in Ireland was produced in Belfast. In the same year, the passing of the Act to Prevent the Further Growth of Popery targeted not just Catholics but Presbyterians in office, a discrimination which remained in place until 1780. Nevertheless, the Presbyterian religion remained vibrant, with fierce tensions continuing between its adherents and the Church of Ireland, and with many Presbyterians considerably richer than their Anglican counterparts. In records from these times, it is worth noting that the word 'Protestant' more usually refers to followers of the Church of Ireland, with Presbyterians noted as 'Dissenters', from an English perspective.

In the 1720s, the trade of brown or unbleached linen cautiously commenced in the city, with heavy competition in Lurgan and Newry. Educated society received the *Belfast Newsletter* newspaper from 1737, whilst in 1752 the town's first bank was established. For the poorer side of society, the town's first poor house was constructed in 1774 at Clifton House (p.35). Belfast's population continued to grow, reaching just under 20,000 inhabitants by the early 1790s. At the same time, many of the town's merchant fraternity sought to improve the local infrastructure, particularly with the city's port facilities, and were successful in assuming many of the corporation's responsibilities.

With the textiles traders turning towards trade in bleached lined, using first lime and later sulphuric acid to bleach the cloth, a White Linen Hall was opened in 1783, on the site now occupied by Belfast City Hall. Communications routes were constructed to bring in bleached linen from the surrounding countryside, including the Lagan Canal, built between 1756 and 1793. As the town prospered, a new library opened in 1788 to help cater for its inhabitants' educational needs; the same institution continues today as the Linen Hall Library on Donegall Square (p.35). It is Ireland's last surviving subscription library.

Despite the growing success of the trade, linen weaving itself did not commence in the town until many decades later. Cotton spinning and weaving, established in Belfast from 1777, was seen as a stronger and more favoured competitor, initially giving employment to many at the town's Poor House, before becoming a major industry in the town at large.

Rebellion and union

By the late eighteenth century, change was in the air. The American colonies went through a revolutionary war from 1776 to 1783, and broke away to form the United States. Many Ulster Presbyterians had contributed to the American cause, having emigrated from Ireland as a consequence of the Penal Laws and the lure of better prospects. In Belfast, volunteer corps were raised to defend Ireland whilst the British Army was distracted overseas, and its members soon began to seek reform to the Irish Parliament. Amongst their complaints were the anti-democratic means for electing members from the corporation to represent them at Parliament, and the continued discrimination against Roman Catholics.

The French Revolution of 1789 was widely celebrated by Presbyterians in Belfast. Soon their zeal for reform went further, following publications by Theobold Wolfe Tone, a Dublin-based lawyer, and Thomas Paine, defending the ideas of the revolution on the Continent. In October 1791, the first branch of the Society of United Irishmen, an oath-bound society, was formed in the town by three Presbyterians: Henry Joy McCracken, Samuel Neilson and Thomas Russell, which soon spread across Ireland. Its guiding republican principles were drafted to ensure a unity amongst the people of Ireland, to counter England's influence over the country, reform of the Irish Parliament, and the removal of sectarian barriers between those of all faiths in the service of Ireland.

In June 1795, McCracken, Neilson and Russell met with Wolfe Tone at McArt's Fort on Cave Hill to plan a rebellion to fulfil their aims. Their zeal for national reform in Presbyterian Belfast was not matched by some of their brethren in other parts of the country, with Protestants in more isolated communities organising to form the Orange Order in 1795, in the aftermath of ongoing skirmishes fought between the Catholic 'Defenders' and the Protestant 'Peep o' day Boys'. Finding common cause with the Catholic Defenders, the United Irishmen finally rose in rebellion in the north and the south in 1798 but were heavily defeated. Several leaders were executed, including McCracken, who was hanged outside the Market House of Belfast. Martial law, declared in the city from May 1798, lasted just a year.

As a consequence of the failed rebellion, Ireland was brought into the United Kingdom of Great Britain and Ireland from 1 January 1801. With the abolition of the Irish Parliament, Belfast was now represented by a single MP at the British Parliament in Westminster, England.

In the late eighteenth century, Irish Catholics started to settle in Belfast. A census of the town in 1782 showed 365 Catholics in residence, who mostly worshipped in the open air at Friar's Bush. Just two years later,

Queen's Bridge, over the River Lagan.

on 30 May 1784, St Mary's at Chapel Lane hosted its first service, led by Father Hugh O'Donnell. The construction of this building was funded by the 'Handsome Collection' gathered by Presbyterians and Anglicans at their own church services across the town.

By 1829, when full Catholic Emancipation had been granted finally by the British Parliament, almost a third of Belfast's inhabitants were Roman Catholic. Friar's Bush graveyard, the oldest burial site in Belfast, was extended and consecrated as the Catholic community's main cemetery, with thousands buried there during the 1830s cholera epidemic, and the Great Famine (*an Gorta Mór*) of the 1840s. In 1869, Milltown Cemetery opened as the main burial ground for the Catholic community in west Belfast, in a role that continues to this day.

The Famine

Belfast was not immune to the Famine from 1845 to 1851, with many of the town's working-class population, both Protestant and Catholic, equally affected by the blight that hit the potato, in addition to the rise of prices in other foods. As Belfast's Board of Guardians struggled to

TIP: An interesting article on Belfast's experience of the Famine, by Dr Christine Kinealy of the Ireland's Great Hunger Institute at Quinnipiac University, can be read at **https://bit.ly/BelfastFamine**.

cope, soup kitchens were created in places such as Ballymaccarrett and Smithfield, to help feed thousands a day – not just its own resident population, but also the many arriving daily to seek relief from the countryside.

Industrial Belfast

Throughout the nineteenth century, Belfast's population continued to grow, with the new union benefiting both its merchants and industries. In 1831, the town's population reached 53,000 inhabitants, by 1841 it was at 71,447, in 1861 it reached 121,602, and by 1901 there had been a huge increase to 349,180. Many industries emerged in nineteenth-century Belfast, from rope making and engineering works, to whiskey and tobacco manufacturing. By far the largest employers, however, remained the textiles industries, and from the middle of the century onwards, the shipbuilding industry.

By the 1830s, the cotton mills were giving way to the manufacture of linen, with damask weaving, established in the Ardoyne from 1825, soon gaining a worldwide reputation. With the advent of mechanisation in the latter half of the century, much larger and more productive mills were established, such as that of the York Street Flax Spinning Company at

Henry Street (p.141). With the supply of cotton from the southern states of the USA cut off during the American Civil War from 1861 to 1865, the production of Belfast linen rapidly accelerated, and remained a major employer until well into the twentieth century.

As Belfast thrived, its governance evolved. A more democratic council was established in 1842, with a mayor, ten aldermen, and thirty councillors elected to take over the town's administrative functions. To service the import of raw materials for the textiles trades, and the export of its products, a shipbuilding industry was developed, in an area that previously had a limited shipbuilding tradition, despite the creation of the first regular shipyard in 1791, run by

The Famine window inside Belfast City Hall.

William Ritchie and others. Belfast was not a natural location for such an industry, but what it did have was a readily available workforce, which attracted entrepreneurial investors sensing an opportunity. To assist with industry, the Belfast Harbour Commission dredged the River Lagan and constructed yards on reclaimed land adjacent to deep water channels within the lough. Soon the yards were pioneering construction techniques on iron hulls, and from the 1880s onwards, steel vessels.

In 1854, Edward James Harland purchased one of these yards, and in 1861 partnered with Gustav Wilhelm Wolff to create a new firm that would dominate shipbuilding for decades. Harland and Wolff (p.141) was soon a household name around the world, not least for its constructions for the famous White Star Line, which serviced the transatlantic routes. In May 1911, its most famous vessel, the RMS *Titanic*, was launched. The twin cranes of Samson and Goliath, built on the Harland and Wolff yard on Queen's Island between 1969 and 1974, today remain an internationally recognised symbol of both the industry and the modern city itself. Competing alongside Harland and Wolff were two other Belfast shipbuilding firms: MacIlwaine and Lewis, created in 1868 by John MacIlwaine and Richard Lewis, which later became MacIlwaine and McColl from 1889 (with Hector McColl as a partner), and Workman Clark and Company, founded in 1881 by Frank Workman and George Clark, which took over the MacIlwaine and McColl yard in 1893.

The City of Belfast's coat of arms.

In the early 1850s, the third Marquess of Donegall was forced to sell off most of the family estate in and around Belfast through the Encumbered Estates Court, to pay off his father's substantial debts. Within the next few years, the borough's boundaries were significantly expanded beyond those of the original charter town. In 1888, Belfast was granted city status by Queen Victoria, and two years later received its coat of arms, with the motto *Pro tanto quid retribuamus*, taken from Psalm 116, meaning 'What shall we give back in return for so much?' The City Hall was built in 1906.

In 1896, a further boundary extension saw the city grow to an area some 23 square miles in size. Hundreds of new, long streets were created, comprising 'kitchen houses' and 'parlour houses', for the largely immigrant working population. The city's infrastructure was further developed with trams, widened streets, new public conveniences and sewerage facilities. The city centre, as we know it today, was defined by the creation of Royal Avenue in the 1880s.

TIP: Good examples of Belfast's Victorian kitchen and parlour houses have been preserved at McMaster Street by the Hearth Historic Buildings Trust. See **https://bit.ly/McMasterStreet**.

A divided city

As the population grew through the nineteenth century, so too did sectarian conflict between the town's Protestant and Catholic communities, with many now seeking membership in Orange lodges and Ribbonmen societies to defend their interests, and occasionally clashing in riots. Attempts were made in the 1820s to ban such organisations, as well as in the aftermath of Emancipation, but sectarianism became embedded. Following serious rioting over the next few decades, in particular in 1857 and 1864, the town's police service was replaced with members of the Royal Irish Constabulary, most of whom were Catholic and from the south of Ireland.

Support for the Orange Order within the Protestant communities grew, and from 1870 a right to march was granted; at the same time, a parallel organisation, the Ancient Order of Hibernians, created a similar conduit for the Catholic community. By the end of the century, the two main religious traditions were firmly polarised on political lines as the fight for Home Rule commenced, with nationalists, most of whom were Catholic, in favour, and unionists, who were largely Protestant, opposed.

The twentieth century

By the beginning of the twentieth century, Belfast was a city with a substantial working-class majority, managed by white collar workers within the major industries.

On one front, however, a substantial part of the workforce in Belfast, namely the city's women, still did not have the vote. In 1872, the North of Ireland Women's Suffrage Society had been formed in Belfast by Isabella Tod, to be later renamed the Irish Women's Suffrage Society from 1909. Although a minor victory had been secured with regards to local government elections in 1887, with qualifying electors redefined as 'persons' rather than 'men', universal suffrage was still years away from realisation, and thus the campaign continued, with frustration eventually leading to more militant tactics. In one example, the *Northern Whig* on 13 February 1913 described how a viscous black fluid had been found maliciously poured into a letterbox at the General Post Office on Royal Avenue in an attempt to destroy its contents, one of many attacks on letterboxes across the city. Arrested suffragettes went on hunger strike, prompting the government to force feed them via the 'Cat and Mouse Act'.

On another front was the issue of workers' rights. In 1907, Liverpool-born trade unionist 'Big' Jim Larkin, a member of the National Union of Dock Labourers, led the transport and dock workers of Belfast to strike for better pay and conditions. In 1909, Larkin established the Irish Transport and General Workers Union, and appointed James Connolly to lead the Belfast branch. Both men would temporarily bring the nation's capital to its knees with the Dublin Lockout in 1913, whilst Connolly would be executed just three years later for his part in the Easter Rising, as leader of the Irish Citizen Army.

With the city's middle-class Protestant communities at an economic advantage to their Catholic neighbours in many regards, the nationwide agitation for political change continued, as a third

The author's great-grandfather Ernest Graham (1893–1942) served as a signaller with the Royal Engineers in the First World War.

attempt to deliver Home Rule was pursued at Westminster. On 11 April 1912 a third Home Rule Bill was published, something long feared by the majority of the Protestant Unionist population. This resulted in a protest on 28 September 1912, designated as 'Ulster Day' by the Ulster Unionist Council, at which thousands of men signed the 'Ulster Covenant', and women a parallel 'Declaration of Loyalty' (p.99). At City Hall, 250,000 gathered to pledge their support. In its immediate aftermath, the Ulster Volunteer Force was founded as an anti-Home Rule Protestant militia, with the nationalist Irish Volunteers formed in response. As all hell was set to break loose in a possible civil war, the First World War broke out, pausing everything.

Some 46,000 volunteers from both sides of the divide in the city, including 3,000 reservists from the shipyards, were called to service for the war. Many served within the 36th (Ulster) Division and the 16th (Irish) Division, whilst others engaged in different services, including the Royal Navy and Merchant Navy. On the home front, some 37,000 labourers were employed in wartime shipbuilding in the Belfast yards, whilst at James Mackie & Sons ('Mackies'), a textiles machinery manufacturer on the Springfield Road, workers were moved over to the manufacture of some 75 million shells.

The northern capital
In 1919, a strike saw 60,000 Protestant and Catholic workers in Belfast down tools for almost a month; in the same year a war of independence was launched by republicans wishing to see Ireland free of the United Kingdom. In July 1920, the unity in the shipyards was shattered, as Edward Carson called for 'non-loyal' workers to be expelled. Over the next few weeks, some 11,000 workers, mostly Roman Catholic, but also Protestant labour activists, were driven from the shipyards, factories and mills. These actions, with their inevitable retaliations, led to some 500 deaths across the city. The unionist-dominated press focused on the outrages against Protestant communities, whilst attacks against Catholics and nationalists were documented by Father John Hasson of St Mary's at Chapel Lane, and published in a book called *Facts and Figures of the Belfast Pogrom 1920–1922*. Sponsored by Michael Collins, the book was withdrawn from publication in 1922 by the government in Dublin following his death, and did not see publication again until 1997. As a consequence of the trouble, a 'Belfast Boycott' was followed across much of the new Free State

In its midst of all the chaos, the Government of Ireland Act of 1920 led to the Partition of Ireland a year later in 1921, and the creation of Northern

Ireland, with Belfast now its capital city. With the catastrophic loss of the Public Record Office in Dublin in the ensuing civil war in 1922, a new national archive was established in Belfast a year later, called the Public Record Office of Northern Ireland (p.24), whilst a separate General Register Office was also established in Belfast for civil registration purposes (p.23).

> **TIP:** For interesting tales of city life between 1918 and 1939 visit the 'Belfast Between the Wars' website at **www.belfastbetweenthewars. com.**

The Second World War

Now part of Northern Ireland, Belfast advanced on a few fronts, not least with the Education Act of 1923, which led to a new schools' building programme. Productivity was maintained in its key industries of linen and shipbuilding, but by the 1930s, with a worldwide depression and other international factors, output slowly began to fall. Despite high unemployment, firms such as the tobacco giants Gallahers, and plane builders Short Brothers, still employed thousands. By 1937, the census recorded some 438,000 inhabitants in the city.

On 3 September 1939, the United Kingdom declared war against Germany. In Belfast, many volunteered to sign up, whilst civilians and industry switched to a wartime manufacturing footing and economy. The government carried out an emergency census on 29 September to create a National Identity Register (p.101), through which identity cards could be issued, and should it be needed, a list be made available for a potential draft.

At first, the City Corporation did not take seriously the threat of a German attack on Belfast, deeming the German bombers not to have sufficient range. That assumption was destroyed utterly in 1941 on 7 April, 15 April, and again on 4 May, when devastating Blitz attacks were rained down on to the city by the Luftwaffe (p.151).

The Troubles and beyond

Following the war, the linen industry continued to decline, but Harland and Wolff experienced a construction boom until the late 1950s, before it too began to experience a slowing down with its order books. Nevertheless, employment across Belfast remained high.

By the late 1960s, sectarianism had again raised its head, with the outbreak of the 'Troubles' leading to a thirty-year military and paramilitary campaign between the forces of the British Government and the Provisional IRA. Belfast paid dearly during these years, with outrage upon outrage inflicted by loyalist and republican paramilitaries against each other, and towards many innocents caught up in the carnage. The Northern Irish Government was finally suspended in 1972, but in Belfast, so too was its long-standing corporation, with local government reforms leading to the creation of Belfast City Council from 1973.

In 1998, the Good Friday Agreement finally paved the way towards an enduring peace. The sun finally returned to Belfast, which continues to prosper under its gaze.

Chapter 2

OUT FOR A DANDER

Before looking into our ancestors' lives, a fair bit of orientation may at first be required to get a sense of the lay of the land.

Historically, the peoples of Belfast arrived to the city from three main areas: Ireland, Scotland and England; all of them with their own speech patterns, mannerisms and cultures. In many ways, across time these have melded to create a common character for the city's folk, and yet on many fronts they have also been preserved and vigorously defended, most notably through the religions and politics with which they have expressed their identities.

Whilst Belfast's folk may have lived in the same places throughout their lives, how the authorities tried to administer to their needs changed massively over time, from the requirements of poor relief administration to the boundaries of electoral wards for elections.

In this chapter, I will describe two key areas to get to grips with when trying to understand Belfast: the administrative divisions of governance, and the very languages that are spoken by its people.

Administrative boundaries
As noted in Chapter 1, Belfast has evolved over hundreds of years, growing to become the large metropolitan area that we know today. However, in terms of administrative boundaries, there is a lot more to how records were collated for the area than the single word 'Belfast' can imply.

Historically, in Ireland there has been a changing hierarchy of divisions into which various administrative tasks were performed, summarised in the following diagram:

You had the island of Ireland, subdivided into four provinces, each of which was then divided into counties. These were further subdivided

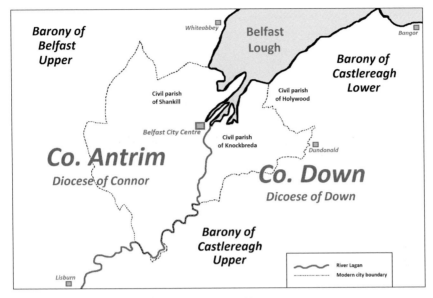

Some of the key administrative units affecting Belfast.

into baronies (and 'half-baronies'), and then into civil parishes, sharing the same boundaries as Church of Ireland parishes, each of which in turn comprised a variety of townlands, the smallest administrative unit. Whilst today we simply add a postcode to the end of addresses in Belfast to specify their position, for older periods it is often essential to know which townland your family was based within.

All of these various boundaries were used for different purposes. Grand juries (p.136) were drawn up to administer to baronies, which were also the land units used in the seventeenth-century Plantations through which settlers were settled. Parishes had ecclesiastical roles for the state church, the Church of Ireland (p.68), but also some roles for the repair and maintenance of civil infrastructure, through its vestries.

This all worked well and good until the nineteenth century appeared, at which point the state decided to get a bit more creative, as new challenges emerged. In July 1838, an 'Act for the more effectual Relief of the Destitute Poor in Ireland' was passed to set up a new poor relief system in the country. To administer this, the country was carved up into a series of 'poor law unions', which respected none of the administrative boundaries that had previously existed, and which instead co-existed in parallel alongside them. In turn, these poor law unions were used as the basis for what became known as 'superintendent registrars' districts' (p.55) when the civil registration of births and deaths system commenced in 1864. Just for good measure, another unit emerged from the poor law unions known as 'district electoral divisions', for elections and census-gathering purposes. In 1898, the use of civil parishes and baronies was finally abolished in favour of these poor law unions and their derivatives, which continued in use in Northern Ireland until 1948.

On top of this were other administrative divisions. Roman Catholic parishes had different boundaries to those of the Church of Ireland, often being larger and in some cases having very different names to their Anglican counterparts. Both the Church of Ireland and Roman Catholic parishes were also grouped into 'dioceses' and 'arch-dioceses' for ecclesiastical purposes (including the Anglican church courts), and of course, within both churches the boundaries for these were different! Just for good measure, the Presbyterians in Ireland did not employ a parish structure at all, as their ancestors had done in Scotland, instead meeting in 'congregations' at meeting houses.

At the very top, in 1921, 'Ireland' itself ceased to be the national state unit, with Partition leading to the creation of 'Northern Ireland' and 'Southern Ireland', later the 'Irish Free State' from December 1922, and 'Ireland' or the 'Republic of Ireland' from 1949.

So what does all this have to do with Belfast? Absolutely everything! To know where to look for records, you will often need to know what some of these administrative boundaries were in the past, and where they existed. The following ready reckoner should help to decode them:

Country	Belfast was in **Ireland** prior to May 1921, and has been the capital of **Northern Ireland** following the island's partition in that year.	
Province	Belfast is in the province of **Ulster**.	
Counties	The largest part of Belfast is in **County Antrim**, but a sizeable part of the city is also in **County Down**. The border between the two lies along the River Lagan.	
Baronies	The County Antrim side of the city was historically found within the barony of **Belfast Upper**. The County Down side was based within the baronies of **Castlereagh Upper** and **Castlereagh Lower**.	
Parishes (civil/ Church of Ireland)	On the County Antrim side, the civil parish was **Shankill**. On the County Down side we have **Knockbreda** and **Holywood**.	
Townlands	County Antrim*: Ballyaghagan Ballycollin Ballycullo Ballydownfine Ballyfinaghy	County Down*: Ballycloghan Ballydollaghan Ballyhackamore Ballyhanwood Ballylenaghan

Townlands	County Antrim*:	County Down*:
	Ballygammon	Ballymacarret
	Ballygomartin	Ballymaconaghy
	Ballymagarry	Ballymaghan
	Ballymoney	Ballymisert
	Ballymurphy	Ballynafoy / Ballynafeigh
	Ballysillan Lower	Ballynavally / Ballyomulvally
	Derriaghy	Ballyrushboy
	Dunmurry	Braniel
	Edenderry	Breda
	Englishtown	Carnamuck
	Greencastle	Castlereagh
	Killeaton	Cregagh
	Kilmakee	Galwally
	Lagmore	Gilnahirk
	Legoniel	Gortgrib
	Low Wood	Killeen
	Malone Lower	Knock
	Malone Upper	Knockbreckan
	Old Park	Knocknagoney
	Poleglass	Lisnasharragh
	Skegoneill	Multyhogy
	Tom of the Tae-End	Strandtown / Ballimachoris
		Tullycarnet / Tullycarnan
	* This is based on an indicative list sourced from **https:// en.wikipedia.org/wiki/List_of_townlands_in_Belfast**. Note that with the boundaries of Belfast constantly evolving, there will be others – for a fuller exploration visit **www.townlands.ie**.	
Borough	**Belfast**	
Diocese (Church of Ireland)	The County Antrim side of the city is in the diocese of **Connor**. The County Down side is in the diocese of **Down** (now part of Down and Connor). Both are located within the archdiocese of **Armagh**.	
Parishes (Roman Catholic)	The County Antrim side was mainly within the parishes of **Holy Cross** (Ardoyne) and **Greencastle**. The County Down side mainly comprised **Ballymacarrett** (St Matthew's). In Belfast city centre are five main Roman Catholic charges: **St Joseph's** (Dock Street); **St Malachy's** (Alfred Street); **St Mary's** (Chapel Lane); **St Patrick's** (Donegall Street); and **St Peter's** (Derby Street). **Clonard Monastery** was also established just off the Falls Road in the 1890s.	
Diocese (Roman Catholic)	The Diocese of **Down and Connor**, part of the archdiocese of **Armagh**.	

Probate district	The district probate registry for the city from 1858 onwards was **Belfast**. However, prior to Partition in 1921, Belfast residents could also have their estate taken through the probate process at the Principal Probate Registry in Dublin (p.117).
Poor law union	This was simply called **Belfast**, and was bordered by **Antrim** in County Antrim, and **Lisburn** across parts of both Counties Antrim and Down.
Registration districts	From 1845 to Dec 1863, **Belfast** was the registration district for non-Roman Catholic marriages. From Jan 1864, this was repurposed as the **Superintendent Registrar's District (SRD)**. Subordinate to the 'superintendent registrar', local Medical Officers in Belfast were co-opted as localised registrars within the following dispensary district areas, which were to now act also as **Registration Districts (RDs)**: College, Hospital, Cromac, Smithfield, Dock, Falls By the 1880s, Belfast had been organised into the following RDs: Belfast No. 1, 2, 3, 4, 5, 6, 7, 8, 9, 10 Castlereagh No. 1, 2, and 3 From 1899, the boundaries were further revised, as follows: Belfast Urban 1, 2, 3, 4, 5 ,6, 7, 8, 9, 10, 11, 12, 13, 14, 15, 16 Belfast Rural 1, 2, 3, 4 Castlereagh 1, 2, 3 For a guide to the streets covered by these areas, visit Eddie's Extracts at **www.eddiesextracts.com/oextracts/oeurbandistricts.html**. From 1 October 1973, the registration of all births, marriages and deaths in the city became the responsibility of Belfast City Council, at the Registration Office in Belfast City Hall.

TIP: You will occasionally find areas divided into 'upper' and 'lower' parts, e.g. the baronies of Castlereagh Upper and Castlereagh Lower, or the Belfast townlands of Malone Upper and Malone Lower. When looking at a map, with north vaguely pointing in some direction to the top of the page, you will invariably find that the upper part will be found below the lower part. Don't ask!

Language / *Leid* / *Teanga*

The people of Belfast are gifted with an ability to converse – you will often hear the phrase 'he could talk the hind leg off a donkey' or 'she could chew the hind leg off a horse'! And just for good measure, within the city there were three main languages of historical use.

TIP: If unsure of the administrative boundaries for a particular part of the city, many of them will be listed on Form N of the 1901 and 1911 censuses – see p.92. You can also use conversion tools such as the IreAtlas Townland database at **https://thecore.com/seanruad/** and Shane Wilson's various resources at **www.swilson.info** to locate which boundaries certain units fall within.

English

The main language spoken in Belfast today (and historically, going back to its creation as a charter town), is English. However, the local flavour of English has been heavily influenced across time by a variety of factors, not least the separation from Britain by the Irish Sea, and the prevalence of the Irish and Scots languages in the past, both of which loaned the languages words, idioms, and even grammar. The common greeting, 'What about ye?' may employ English words, but it is most definitely a Northern Irish phrase.

There have been several studies about the use of the English language in the city across time, but a fun edition to browse is David Patterson's 1860 work, *The Provincialisms of Belfast and the Surrounding Districts Pointed Out and Corrected*, which is accessible at Google Books via **www.google. co.uk/books/edition/The_Provincialisms_of_Belfast_and_the_Su/ HOisfNpEpw8C**. This not only describes the language as spoken over 150 years ago, it does so with a wonderfully patronising introduction, giving an insight into just how 'erroneous' our local dialect was becoming to the English ear, thanks to the increasing immigration into the city over the previous fifty years. Amongst Patterson's criticisms, he stated that 'in many words, one or more of the proper sounds or letters are exchanged for other, and therefore improper sounds,' and noted amongst his examples 'eedyet', for 'idiot', 'Proddisin' for Protestant and 'Paypish' for 'Papist'. At times though, even Patterson yielded to some of the sheer melody of the local lingo, noting with amusement what he described as 'English words improperly applied', such as 'a wee *taste* of dirt of your shoe', ' a *terrible* nice mornin'', and 'a *right* rascal'!

You will occasionally come across such idiomatic phrases in historical records, particularly in newspapers where you may find reported speech as given, which can be a joy to read many decades later. To give a small example, a newspaper account of a murder trial held in Belfast in 1875 recorded the testimony of a five times great-uncle of mine from Templepatrick, called David Bill. David's niece had been murdered at his house whilst he had been away to Belfast for the day, and it was he who had found her body and alerted the police. When asked if he had been questioned by the police on the day about the suspect, his nephew William, he replied with a classic Ulsterism, 'Oh, till I was near turned in the head!', which was blunt and to the point.

TIP: Never say 'Yer ma' to someone to get out of a situation in Belfast!

Ulster Scots (Ullans)

Ulster Scots is the Scots language brought to the province from Scotland during the seventeenth-century Plantations, and is sometimes referred to as 'Lallans', the Scots word for 'lowlands', or by the hybrid term 'Ullans' (Ulster Lallans). A background resource for the language is available at **www.ulsterscotsagency.com/what-is-ulster-scots/language**.

For much of its history, Belfast – or *'Bilfawst'* in Scots – was dominated by Presbyterian Scottish settlers who brought their language or *'leid'* with them. They continued to trade and interact with their Scottish brethren in nearby Ayrshire, Argyll, Glasgow and south-west Scotland, just over the *'Sheuch'*, the North Channel in the Irish Sea between Scotland and Ireland. In 1780, the Dublin-based Surveyor of Excise, Amyas Griffith, noted on a visit to Belfast that 'the common people speak broad Scotch, and the better sort differ vastly from us, both in accent and language.'

As with Irish, Scots influenced much of the English spoken in the city; one of the most popular words in use in Belfast is 'crack' meaning 'fun', derived from the Scots *'crak'* or *'crek'*, meaning 'conversation', and carried over to the Irish language as *'craic'*.

A specific dictionary for Ulster Scots can be found online at **www. ulsterscotsacademy.com/words/dictionary/index.php**, whilst James Fenton's *The Hamely Tongue: A Personal Record of Ulster-Scots in County Antrim* provides another excellent dictionary of words to be found in more rural parts of County Antrim, including sources from East Antrim and Kilbride, just beyond the city.

The Ulster Scots Agency (**www.ulsterscotsagency.com**), styled in Scots as 'Tha Boord o Ulster Scotch', is based at the Corn Exchange, 31 Gordon Street, Belfast, and is tasked with promoting the study, conservation, development and use of Ulster Scots as a living language.

The ground floor of the Corn Exchange building hosts the Discover Ulster Scots Centre (**https://discoverulsterscots.com**). Open daily, it offers various displays about the language, as well as gifts and publications for sale. The centre's website also offers many resources about the language, culture and traditions of the Ulster Scots in Belfast, such as the Belfast's Bonnie Burns section at **https://discoverulsterscots. com/language-literature/belfasts-bonnie-burns**, detailing the family connections between the Scottish poet Robert Burns and Belfast, as well as an examination of other poets from the city using the Scots language.

A guide to Ulster Scots place names in Belfast is available at **https:// discoverulsterscots.com/places-interest/ulster/place-names-belfast**

> **TIP:** If you can't find the meaning of an Ulster Scots word from the resources mentioned, try the Scottish-based *Dictionary of the Scots Language* at **https://dsl.ac.uk.**

Irish (Gaeilge)

Belfast has a long and noble tradition on the Irish Gaelic language, in which the language itself is referred to as 'Gaeilge'. Although historically viewed as the language of Catholic Ireland, nothing is ever quite so black and white; some of the Protestant settlers to the north of Ireland during the Ulster Plantations were Scottish Gaelic (Gàidhlig) speakers, whilst many families changed religions in the cause of social advancement during the time of the Penal Laws. Surnames beginning with 'Mac' (and its abridged variation 'Mc'), lay testimony to these older Gaelic origins, with the word 'mac' meaning 'son of' in the language.

In Belfast today, the main cultural centre for Irish language speakers and activists is the Cultúrlann McAdam Ó Fiaich (**www.culturlann.ie**) on the Falls Road. This was named after the Roman Catholic Cardinal Tomas Ó Fiaich (1923–1990), and a nineteenth-century Belfast-based Presbyterian folklorist, antiquarian and Irish language activist, Robert Shipboy McAdam (1808–1895), who did much to preserve aspects of the language from the period. Turas (**www.ebm.org.uk/turas**), based at the East Belfast Mission of the Methodist Church on the Newtownards Road, is a further project seeking to reconnect Protestant learners with this Gaelic heritage.

As well as influencing some of the English vernacular in the city, Gaelic is most commonly found in Belfast through place names, many of which have been anglicised, not least the name of the city itself. A useful site to find the origins of many Irish place names in the city is the Northern Irish Placenames Project at **www.placenamesni.org**. For example, the parish of Shankill comes from '*sean chill*', meaning 'old church', Malone derives from '*maigh luain*', likely meaning 'Luan's plain', whilst the Falls Road, known in Irish as '*Bothar na bhFál*', derives from '*tuath na bhFál*', meaning the 'territory of the enclosures'.

The Cultúrlann McAdam Ó Fiaich, an Irish language centre on the Falls Road.

The Ulster dialect of Irish, including that spoken in Belfast, shares much in common with Scottish Gaelic. To give an example, down south you might hear *'Cad is ainm duit?'* to mean 'What is your name?', but in Belfast you will more likely hear *'Cad é an t-ainm atá ort?'* for the same question, which is closely related to the Scottish equivalent, *'Dè an t-ainm a th' ort?'*. To help understand the language, Google Translate (**https://translate.google.co.uk**) can help to convert texts from Irish to English, whilst online dictionaries and pronunciation guides can be found at **www.teanglann.ie/en**.

TIP: A good starting point to pick up the local dialect of Ulster Irish is the *Now You're Talking* TV series, available online via YouTube (programme 1 is at **https://youtu.be/7nz—LpYC30**). A book with the same title accompanies the series.

Chapter 3

BELFAST'S GUARDIANS AND GATEKEEPERS

There are many excellent archives, libraries and museums in Belfast acting as guardians and gatekeepers for the records which can reveal our ancestral stories. Some of these are professional state-funded or independent repositories, whilst others are run by volunteer groups, societies and research agencies.

In this chapter, I will discuss who they are, what they can offer, and some of the resources that they hold which might help with your research in the city.

General Register Office for Northern Ireland (GRONI)
NISRA, Colby House, Stranmillis Court, Belfast, BT9 5RR
www.nidirect.gov.uk/articles/introduction-groni-and-its-records
Email: gro_nisra@finance-ni.gov.uk
Tel: 0300 200 7890

GRONI is the organisation that is responsible for the registration of all vital events in Northern Ireland, such as births, adoptions, marriages, civil partnerships, divorces, civil partnership dissolutions, and deaths. GRONI was established in Northern Ireland after Partition in 1921, but it is in fact a successor agency to the much earlier established General Register Office of Ireland, which continues to be responsible for registration in the Republic. Today, GRONI forms part of the Northern Ireland Statistics and Research Agency, and is based at Colby House, Stranmillis Court, Belfast, next to the Lyric Theatre.

The civil registration certificates generated by GRONI are the most important set of records when getting started with your research, and how they can do so is explored in Chapter 5. Many of the records of births, marriages and deaths are available online via its website at **https://geni. nidirect.gov.uk**, with closure periods in place for the most recent records (for privacy purposes). However, if you live in Belfast, or can easily get to the city, you can book a visit to GRONI's public search room at Colby House to search the records, using your same online account, or at the Public Record Office of Northern Ireland at Titanic Quarter (p.25).

To book an appointment, visit **https://geni.nidirect.gov.uk/ Appointments** and fill in the online form. The normal opening hours at the time of writing are Mondays to Fridays from 9 a.m. to 4.45 p.m., but check the website for up-to-date details.

Public Record Office of Northern Ireland (PRONI)
2 Titanic Boulevard, Belfast, BT3 9HQ
www.nidirect.gov.uk/proni (also www.nidirect.gov.uk/campaigns/public- record-office-northern-ireland-proni)
Email: proni@communities-ni.gov.uk
Tel: 028 9053 4800

In 1923, a year after the destruction of Ireland's national archive during the Civil War, the Public Record Office of Northern Ireland (PRONI) was established in Belfast to serve as the main archival repository for the

The Reading Room of the Public Record Office of Northern Ireland.

newly created state of Northern Ireland. Under the eyes of its first deputy keeper, D. A. Chart, a former employee of the Public Record Office in Dublin, efforts were made to collect substitutes for much of the material lost concerning the north, including records sourced from solicitors, businesses, politicians, the gentry and the aristocracy. As well as bringing in national government and court records for Northern Ireland, PRONI also collects local government records. Today, at its Titanic Quarter base, the archive offers a wonderful service to those seeking to research their family history on a wide variety of fronts.

PRONI is open five days a week from Monday to Friday. Upon arrival, you will need to apply for a Visitor Pass, which will require you to bring photographic ID. The pass will be valid for ten years, and will allow you to gain access to the Search Room and the Reading Room. Importantly, you cannot order up historical documents without one. For those aged 14–18, where photographic ID may be an issue, there is a special registration facility, details for which are on the website. Once you have your Visitor Pass card, you swipe it at a reader by the main reception desk to register that you are in the building.

> **TIP:** If you have bags and coats that you do not wish to carry around, there are some lockers on the ground floor just across from the reception desk. You can get a token to use the lockers from the main reception desk. There is also a cafe if you need a quick refreshment or some lunch later in the day.

When you are good to go, make your way up to the Search Room on the first floor; if you have infants or children under 14 with you, they are welcome to accompany you. Once you reach the entrance to the Search Room, you swipe your card at the reader by the door, and it will then open. Throughout the Search Room there are a variety of resources available. You will see a series of computer terminals before you on two sides of the room, but the most important starting point for newcomers will almost certainly be the main reception desk, located about halfway along the room to your left. Here you can discuss with the archivists what you are hoping to achieve, and they will happily help you to get started.

At the furthest end of the room is the self-service microfilm reading area. This contains several microfilm readers, and a couple of printers, where you can view microfilms that are stored in the large drawer cabinet that separates the area away from the computers. These seats do not need to be booked but at busy times you may find that you have to wait for one to become available. On tables by the walls next to this area you will see various bound folders that contain printed copies of finding aid resources, such as the *PRONI Guide to Church Records* (p.68), necessary to help you identify the microfilms that you will need.

> **TIP:** PRONI's help guides are also available online via the archive's website. There is an excellent free Wi-Fi service available throughout the building.

Close to the microfilms area there is a library, with some books on the history of Belfast and Northern Ireland, but predominantly finding aids for a range of resources. These include a series of wills calendars for Northern Ireland (many of them not online), gravestone inscription books, and much more. There are also trade directories, maps, and a whole host of other resources.

The main computers in the room are there to provide access to the PRONI catalogue, and to records that have digitised by the archive. It is at these terminals that you can order up documents to be viewed next door in the Reading Room; you will need your Visitor Pass for this, using your unique user number when making any requests. A few terminals also offer additional services to subscription-based genealogy and history websites, as well as the GRONI records platform (p.63).

Once you have ordered your documents, you will need to wait a few minutes for them to be retrieved from storage, and you can then view them in the Reading Room, located on the same floor. Before entering the room, you will see an area called the 'Collection Point'. The records are picked up from here, although not from this window! Instead, you can ask questions of the staff here, and buy cards with credits on them for the use with the large digital scanners in the Search Room. To actually pick up the documents you will need to go into the Search Room and retrieve them from a service area at the side of the Collection Point. You will be asked to sign a short form, essentially agreeing to the archive's rules on copyright, before having any documents handed over to you, at which point you then make your way to the table that you have been allocated.

Each table in the Reading Room has sockets, should you wish to plug in a laptop. You can photograph the documents with your phone, or use the large dedicated scanners in the room, where you can image them and save them straight on to a USB thumb drive. If you need to consult the catalogue again whilst in the Search Room, there are computer terminals at the rear of the room.

The PRONI website

The PRONI website at **www.nidirect.gov.uk/proni** details everything that the archive offers to the public, as well as hosting guides to records, an online catalogue, and several free-to-access digitised records collections. There are detailed instructions on how to get to the archive, its opening hours, how to obtain a Visitor Pass, and news on forthcoming events.

PRONI's online e-catalogue looks different from the version that you will find at the archive itself, with a much more simplistic interface. On a first visit to the institution, you will need an archivist to demonstrate the on-site version of the catalogue for you.

> **TIP:** If you cannot visit the archive, accessing the simpler catalogue from home will still help you to identify documents that you can hire a local genealogist or record agent to consult for you, or from which you can ask PRONI to make copies on your behalf. If planning to go yourself, plan your day's research ahead of your visit by using the catalogue from home to identify holdings of interest, rather than leave it until you arrive. This will give you more time to do research on site.

There are many useful records available at the facility itself, but the archive's online platform can be an incredibly useful research tool for Belfast-themed resources, including the following:

- *Freeholders' records:* This includes searchable lists of voters from across Ulster, with some records for Belfast in the early to mid-nineteenth century (see p.106).
- *Name Search:* This database contains a mix of four datasets, of which only two contain names of folk listed from Belfast.

Included amongst the '1775 Dissenters' Petitions' from Counties Antrim and Down are 191 names of people signing themselves as being from Belfast, who protested against an Irish Parliament law banning Presbyterians from attending Church of Ireland vestry meetings, a law which was later repealed as a consequence. The original petitions have not survived, only transcripts recorded by genealogist Tenison Groves before the destruction of the Public Record Office in Dublin in 1922 (held at PRONI under T808/15307). The 'Pre-1858 Wills and Admons' dataset also includes names of Belfast folk who had a will probated prior to 1858, most of which have not survived (see p.116).

- *PRONI Historical Maps viewer:* This allows you to view five historical Ordnance Survey maps for the north of Ireland, including Belfast, from 1832 to 1963, as well as two later twentieth-century maps. See p.107.
- *Street directories:* This contains twenty-seven searchable volumes from the nineteenth century, covering Belfast and the province of Ulster. See p.103.
- *Ulster Covenant:* A searchable database of signatories to the Ulster Covenant and Declaration of Loyalty in 1912. See p.99.
- *Valuation Revision Books:* A series of registers showing annual revisions made to the ownership and occupation of properties in Belfast and the north following Griffith's Valuation (p.109), and continuing up to 1930.
- *Will Calendars:* A summary for most probate cases from 1858 to 1965 for the three Irish district probate registries for the north prior to Partition, and for Northern Ireland after. See p.117.

There are other digitised Belfast resources available on the site not quite so easily found. For example, the e-catalogue hosts the digitised volume of the 1827 tithe applotment book for the parish of 'Shankhill' (sic) under FIN/5/A/36. This includes details of the lands held within twenty-eight townlands, the names of occupiers, the amount of land held, and the tithe composition payable to the Church of Ireland. Books for Knockbreda (FIN/5/A/195A-B) and Holywood (FIN/5/A/153) are also available.

National Archives of Ireland / *An Chartlann Náisiúnta*
Bishop Street, Dublin 8, Ireland
www.nationalarchives.ie

The successor to the PRO in Dublin today, the National Archives of Ireland (NAI) has various resources that can also help with Belfast-based research.

The archive's main website offers many research guides concerning its holdings, but of particular interest to family historians is the archive's dedicated genealogy platform at **www.genealogy.nationalarchives.ie**. The site's following collections contain material for Belfast:

- Census of Ireland, 1901 and 1911, and pre-1901 survivals
- Census Search Forms, 1841–51
- Soldiers' Wills, 1914–1918
- Calendars of Wills and Administrations, 1858–1922
- Prerogative and diocesan copies of some wills and indexes to others, 1596–1858

- Diocesan and Prerogative Marriage Licence Bonds Indexes, 1623–1866
- Catholic qualification & convert rolls, 1700–1845
- Valuation Office house, field, tenure and quarto books 1824–1856
- Shipping agreements and crew lists, 1863–1921
- Will Registers 1858–1900

Virtual Record Treasury
https://virtualtreasury.ie

The Virtual Record Treasury of Ireland is a valiant project led by the NAI to try to reconstruct and retrieve much of the material lost in the PRO fire in 1922, during the opening salvos of the Irish Civil War. (see p.69). The NAI has worked with many key partners on this, including PRONI and the UK's National Archives in England.

As part of the project, an 'Inventory of Loss' was created, detailing what has not survived, and a separate 'Inventory of Survival', showing what has been reconstructed or retrieved from other sources. As well as being catalogued, surviving records from the fire have been digitised by the team for the first time and added to the site; already created digitised copies by partner institutions may have been supplied to the project, and links for many catalogued entries connect to such records on the platforms of core partners. The project is ongoing, with new content being continually added.

At the time of writing, carrying out a simple test search on the word 'Belfast' produces 794 results. Within these are seventeenth-century digitised leases from the National Archives of Ireland, colour-scanned entries from the Registry of Deeds (p.112), nineteenth-century correspondence from PRONI, historical maps, published material produced by the original PRO in Dublin, Chancery rolls, business records, Parliamentary material, Central Bank of Ireland accounts, and so much more. As such, this is one of those sites where it will undoubtedly be worth a 'lucky dip' search to try to find something connected to your ancestry – you might well be lucky.

TIP: Never assume that Belfast resources are only held at PRONI! There are three national archives worth plundering for the city – PRONI in Belfast, the National Archives in Dublin, and for UK-wide records, such as civil service and military collections, the National Archives at Kew, London (**www.nationalarchives.gov.uk**).

North of Ireland Family History Society

Unit C4 Valley Business Centre, 67 Church Road, Newtownabbey, Co. Antrim, BT36 7LS
www.nifhs.org
Email: Secretary@nifhs.org

The North of Ireland Family History Society has ten branches within Northern Ireland, including the Belfast branch, which held its inaugural meeting in the city on Thursday, 24 February 1983. This usually meets monthly from September to May, offering a series of lectures and events to members in the area, both virtually and in person. The branch also has a dedicated page outlining its yearly talks programme, accessible via **www.nifhs.org/branches**, as well as a private Facebook group at **www. facebook.com/groups/502783090618621**. As a member you can attend meetings of any branch, receive copies of the society's journal, as well as its bi-annual E-Newsletter.

> **TIP:** If you live beyond Belfast or Northern Ireland, you can join the society as an 'Associate Member', which will still permit you to join many of the online sessions.

An additional benefit of society membership is free access to the 'Irish Collection' on J-STOR (**www.jstor.org**), with many journals digitised in partnership with Queen's University. These include historical editions of the society's own *North Irish Roots* journal (indexed from 1983 to 2021), and some journals specific to Belfast such as *The Belfast Magazine and Literary Journal* (from 1825), and *The Belfast Monthly Magazine* (1808–1814), with many other titles of interest dating back to the eighteenth century.

Research Centre

The society operates a dedicated research centre in Newtownabbey, located just a couple of miles past Fortwilliam as you drive north on the A6 out of north Belfast. Directions to the premises, and details of when it is open, can be found on the main society website; it may also be possible to book a visit outside of the regular opening hours, if a volunteer is available to assist.

Beyond the main reception of the centre, and the society's main office in the building, are four key facilities which may be useful for your research:

- The Randal Gill Library, named after a former society president and librarian, holds a wealth of useful resources, including many transcribed and indexed datasets, such as church, graveyard and newspaper collections. The room also includes an extensive 'Irish collection' of books, which can only be consulted on site.
- The Irish Journal Room contains a series of journals from various societies in the north of Ireland, including its own journal, *North Irish Roots*, as well as family history magazines from the UK and Ireland.
- The Map Room has copies of 6 inch to the mile Ordnance Survey maps from Northern Ireland, including Belfast, as well as various directories, and the early nineteenth-century Ordnance Survey Memoirs for much of the north. Although Belfast was sadly not surveyed for this, many surrounding parishes were.
- Finally, the Honneyman Room, named after the first president of the society, Dr David Honneyman, is where the society holds regular courses and lectures, covering a range of topics and levels of experience.

A much more detailed discussion of holdings for the various rooms is outlined on the society's website.

TIP: If you cannot get to the research centre in Newtownabbey, the society offers a look-up service for its members, details of which are also available online.

Ulster Historical Foundation
Bradley Thallon House, Unit 44D, Kiltonga Estate, Belfast Road, Newtownards, BT23 4TJ
www.ancestryireland.com
Tel: 028 9181 2073
Email: enquiry@uhf.org.uk

The Ulster Historical Foundation was founded in 1956, and works as an education and non-profit-based research and publishing agency. From 1956 to 1987 it was in fact a part of PRONI, only to become a separate agency in its own right from 1988. Currently based in Newtownards, just a few minutes' drive from Belfast, it offers a variety of services that can help with research into your city forebears.

The Foundation has a society called the Ulster Historical and Genealogical Guild, membership of which provides access to two annual journals: *Familia: Ulster Genealogical Review,* and the *Directory of Irish Family*

History Research, as well as discounts on its publications, research services, and vital records databases. Several hundred additional databases are also freely provided to members. The organisation has a dedicated on-site research and newspaper library, which members are entitled to use.

The following are some of the online databases available with specific reference to Belfast:

- Burials in Milltown Cemetery Public Ground, Belfast, 1869–1895
- A list of those who contributed to the funds of the House of Industry, Belfast, 1834
- List of Subscribers to the 'Historic Memorials of the 1st Presbyterian Church of Belfast', 1887
- Appeal to citizens of Belfast for information on six missing brass cannons, May 1798
- Directory of Businesses in Belfast, 1807
- Directory of Businesses in Belfast, 1808
- Belfast Officials in 1820
- The Belfast Almanack & Directory, 1820
- Belfast Merchants & Tradesmen
- Butchers in Belfast, 1830
- Belfast Cotton Industry, 1819
- Blacksmiths Registered in Belfast, 1833–43
- Search Royal Belfast Academical Institute Alumni, 1814–1875
- Students at Queen's College, Belfast, 1849–59
- Non-Matriculated Students at Queen's College, Belfast, 1849–59
- Principals of Belfast Schools, 1926
- Belfast Leases, 1750–1815
- Persons who Donated Money at Formal Opening of New Mater Hospital, Belfast, 1900
- Contributors to an Envelope Collection for New Mater Hospital, Belfast, 1900
- Subscribers to Building Fund for New Mater Hospital, Belfast, 1894
- Subscribers to charity sermon at opening of new Mater Hospital, Belfast, 1900
- Members of Central Committee appointed in 1894 to raise funds for new Mater Hospital
- Merchants and Traders of Belfast, 1865
- Pawnbrokers of Belfast, 1836
- Belfast Medical Society, Obituaries, 1825–1850
- Inns, Hotels and Taverns in Belfast, 1839
- Names of proprietors of the Belfast Commercial Buildings, 1823

Whilst these illustrate the range of resources available, there are many other datasets also listing Belfast people amongst names from elsewhere in Ulster and / or Ireland. In addition, are the organisation's databases for parish records of births/baptisms, marriages and burials, as well as transcripts of civil records events. In most cases, these include records up to 1899/1900 for a variety of denominations, but of particular note are the extended collections of Roman Catholic baptismal records for many Belfast parishes going up to 1930.

> **TIP:** The Foundation has a substantial publications programme, with its own dedicated bookshop platform at **www.booksireland.org.uk**, selling books, e-books and downloadable publications. Sign up for news of its latest releases at **www.booksireland.org.uk/newsletter**.

Belfast Family History Centre (LDS)
Church of Jesus Christ of Latter-day Saints, 401 Holywood Road, Belfast, BT14 2GU
www.familysearch.org/en/wiki/Belfast_Family_History_Centre,_Northern_Ireland
Tel: 028 9076 8250

The Belfast Family History Centre is part of a worldwide network of FamilySearch centres, and affiliate centres, run by the Church of Jesus Christ of Latter-day Saints (**www.churchofjesuschrist.org**).

The church, headquartered in Salt Lake City, Utah, USA, has a theological requirement for its members to research their ancestry, and has invested heavily in sourcing records from around the world that can assist their efforts. It graciously makes many of these records freely available online (see p.50), but some records are blocked from non-member access due to licensing restrictions, including records that have been digitised in partnership with commercial agencies such as Ancestry and Findmypast (p.47). Such records, however, can be accessed at the church's family history centres, usually for a small donation.

The centre in Belfast is based at the church's Holyrood Road Ward meeting house. It offers regular open days for members and non-

> **TIP:** Other FamilySearch centres, offering similar access, are available worldwide – these can be located through **www.familysearch.org/centers/locations**.

members, and can also be opened by appointment. Check the website for details.

Belfast Central Library

Royal Avenue, Belfast, Antrim, BT1 1EA
www.librariesni.org.uk/libraries/greater-belfast/belfast-central-library/
Tel: 028 9050 9156
Email: belfast.heritage@librariesni.org.uk

Located on Royal Avenue, close to St Anne's Cathedral, Belfast Central Library first opened its doors in 1888, and is still the main public lending library for the city, today being run as part of Libraries NI (**www.librariesni.org.uk**). The facility offers a vast amount of locally published material, as well as items within its Special Collections, which include resources such as school registers and local electoral registers.

The Library has a Heritage section on its second floor, which offers additional materials, from maps and photographs, to newspaper cuttings files and a variety of journals. Amongst its more unique holdings are an extensive collection of street directories (p.103) from the nineteenth and twentieth centuries; a detailed card index to individuals mentioned in the *Belfast Newsletter*; and electoral registers from the twentieth century.

Belfast Central Library.

The Newspaper Library (p.163), accessible from Library Street, also offers a variety of microfilms and original volumes which can be searched, much of which is not available online or in a microform.

Linen Hall Library

17 Donegall Square North, Belfast, BT1 5GB
https://linenhall.com
Tel: 028 9032 1707
Email: info@linenhall.com

Located just across the road from the City Hall, the Linen Hall Library is Belfast's oldest library. Initially founded in 1788 as the Belfast Reading Society, it remains the last remaining subscription library in Ireland. Subscriptions are available for individuals, families and corporate members, as well as concessionary rates for those who are unemployed, retired, students, under-18s, and associate members (those based outside of Northern Ireland who come to the country for less than three months a year). As well as gaining access to all materials on site, members can also gain admission to a members-only area on the second level.

Amongst its many resources, the library's Irish and Local History Collection holds a great deal of material concerning the life of the city, including its own minutes from the Belfast Library and Society for Promoting Knowledge, as well as collections delving into the recent Troubles and beyond. An online catalogue is available at **https://lhlibapp. qub.ac.uk/search~S1**. The library also hosts published family histories, gravestone inscription books for the city, school registers, church records and more.

Past copies of the library's former quarterly journal, *The Linen Hall Review*, from spring 1984 to winter 1989, are available via the J-STOR platform (p.30).

Clifton House

2 North Queen Street / 2 Clifton Street, Belfast, Antrim, BT15 1ES
https://cliftonbelfast.com
Tel: 028 9099 7022
Email: info@CliftonBelfast.org.uk and archive@cliftonbelfast.org.uk

The Belfast Charitable Society was established in 1752 at Clifton House, with the city's Poor House opened by the body in 1774 (p.126). The society's archives contain substantial records for those who may have been admitted to the Poor House and to the later established Old People's

Home from 1882 to 1972. In addition, the Society also established and managed Clifton Street Cemetery (p.84), with many of its records equally available for consultation at the institution.

Visitors are encouraged to attend by appointment, or the society can carry out research for you for a small fee.

Queen's University – The McClay Library and Archive

Special Collections, Floor 1, The McClay Library, 10 College Park, Belfast, BT7 1LP

www.qub.ac.uk/directorates/InformationServices/TheLibrary

The library service and archives of Queen's University hold a vast range of materials concerning the history of the university, back to its original founding as Queen's College in 1845, as well as the history of Belfast and Ireland. Public access is available, although seating priority will always be given to students in pursuit of their studies.

The McClay Library has an online catalogue available for the main library on its home page, and an archive catalogue at **www.calmview.eu/QUB**. The Special Collections department has a digital platform also available at **www.qub.ac.uk/directorates/InformationServices/TheLibrary/SpecialCollections/** with free-to-access resources. The following concern Belfast:

• Archive – Institutional Archive of Queen's University Belfast
• Belfast General Hospital
• Belfast Jewish Gazette (1933–1934)
• Belfast Jewish Record (1954–2002)
• Queen's Film Theatre Brochure Archive (1968–2017)
• Ulad (1904–1905)
• The Irish Song Project (material relating to the Belfast Harpers Festival of 1792)
• Map Collections (a third dealing with Belfast from 1570 to 1900)

Various online exhibitions are available through the website also, including 'Surviving the City: Poverty and Public Health in Belfast, 1888–1914', at **https://omeka.qub.ac.uk/exhibits/show/survivingthecity**, with an accompanying blog at **https://blogs.qub.ac.uk/belfastpovhist**.

Commemorating QUB's involvement in the world wars is a Digitised Book of Remembrance, and an exhibition feature entitled 'Queen's and World War One'.

Ulster University Library Services
Block BC, Cathedral Quarter, Belfast
www.ulster.ac.uk/library

Ulster University is the modern establishment to have evolved from its earlier predecessors, the New University of Ulster, the Ulster Polytechnic, Magee College and the College of Art (where I was a graphic design student from 1989 to 1991!). At the time of writing, its main library services were being relocated from Jordanstown and Belfast to a new facility at Block BC of the Belfast campus. As with QUB, Ulster University's library has extensive holdings, with its online catalogue available at **https://catalogue.library.ulster.ac.uk**.

The university's Special Collections and Rare Books department is not based in Belfast, but at the Magee and Coleraine campuses, with its platform at **https://guides.library.ulster.ac.uk/specialcollections** detailing holdings. There is public access available, with non-student visitors requested to bring identification with them on a visit with details of their name and address.

The university's archive (**www.ulster.ac.uk/library/services/university-archive**) was set up in 2022, with holdings prior to this kept at PRONI (p.24), catalogued under D4327 and NUU.

Historical societies
Belfast has several local history groups which may also help with your research, including the following:

- Belfast Local History Project
  www.belfasthistoryproject.com
- East Belfast Historical Society
  https://sites.google.com/view/eastbelfasthistoricalsociety1/home
- West Belfast Historical Society
  www.westbelfasthistoricalsociety.org.uk
- Shankill Area Social History
  www.facebook.com/Shankill-Area-Social-History-SASH-Group-240223979375644/

Presbyterian Historical Society of Ireland (PHSI)
Assembly Buildings, Fisherwick Place, Belfast, BT1 6DW
www.presbyterianhistoryireland.com
Tel: 028 9041 7299
Email: phsilibrarian@pcinet.org

The Assembly Buildings at Fisherwick Place, home to the Presbyterian Historical Society of Ireland.

If your ancestors were Presbyterian (p.71), the PHSI in Belfast may help on a number of fronts. Established in 1907 by the Presbyterian Church in Ireland, the Non-Subscribing Presbyterian Church of Ireland, and the Reformed Presbyterian Church of Ireland, the mission of the organisation is to 'explore and promote an understanding of the history of Presbyterianism in Ireland', and in all its various flavours.

The society has a substantial library and archive of materials concerning the history of Presbyterianism in Ireland, including detailed histories of individual congregations, copies of Presbyterian registers held at PRONI, and some original church records (see p.72). If you are not sure which Belfast congregation your ancestors attended, a map on the PHSI website pinpoints the locations of each meeting house, its name, and the presbytery to which it adhered.

The society offers four tiers of membership (annual, life, student, and associate), each of which provides access to the members-only area. This includes various online resources, which are outlined at **www.presbyterianhistoryireland.com/web-resources/**, including a Fasti of Presbyterian ministers in Ireland, a First World War Roll of Honour, and various Presbyterian magazines, as well as lists of students at Belfast's Union Theological College (The Presbyterian College) from 1853 to 1953, and the Royal Belfast Academical Institution from 1814 to 1921. Some resources are made freely available on the main website.

It is possible to visit the society's premises to carry out research, but whilst it has an enquiry service, it does not carry out family history research itself. If making a visit, charges will only be made for copying of materials, but as a charitable endeavour, the PHSI is always grateful for any donations that can be made for the use of its services.

> **TIP:** If you're thirsty after visiting the PHSI, or just fancy seeing a gorgeous Victorian establishment, check out Belfast's most famous pub, the historic Crown Liquor Saloon (**www.nationaltrust.org.uk/the-crown-bar**), located about a minute away on Great Victoria Street.

Methodist Historical Society of Ireland
Edgehill House, 9 Lennoxvale, Belfast, BT9 5BY
https://methodisthistoryireland.org

Founded in 1926, the Methodist Historical Society of Ireland has a mission to explain the story of Methodism from its initial establishment in Ireland in 1746. The history of Methodism is as complex as that of the Presbyterian churches, with various flavours of the denomination in existence across time. They are helpfully explained in the society's guide, *Irish Methodist Baptismal and Marriage Records*, available on its website at **https://methodisthistoryireland.org/irish-methodist-baptismal-and-marriage-records/**.

As with the PHSI, there is a library and archive with many unique resources, as well as copies of materials found deposited at PRONI concerning Methodist churches, preaching houses and chapels. The society's resources can be used by the public on two days a week, with details on how to gain access available at **https://methodisthistoryireland.org/plan-your-visit/**.

Many resources are freely available on the society's website, including guides to Methodist ministers and churches. Included within its Irish Methodist Churches database are short histories for fifteen Belfast-based churches: Ballynafeigh, Belvoir, Bloomfield, Cavehill, Cregagh, Donegall Road (two accounts), Grosvenor House, Knock, Lisburn Road, Seymour Hill, Sydenham, Woodvale, Edgehill College, Mountpottinger, and Shankill Road.

Many Methodist records have been microfilmed and digitised for consultation at PRONI (p.24).

Land and Property Services
Lanyon Plaza, 7 Lanyon Place, Town Parks, Belfast, BT1 3LP
www.nidirect.gov.uk/articles/searching-the-land-registry

The agency tasked with handling the Land Registry in Northern Ireland is Land and Property Services (LPS), which operates five customer service centres providing access to entries recorded in the Land Registry following Partition.

The centres can also be used to search for Northern Irish properties registered within the Registry of Deeds from 1923 to 1989 in paper format, and from 1990 onwards in digital format; earlier enquiries will need to be carried out at PRONI, or at the Registry of Deeds in Dublin.

To carry out searches you will need to obtain a permit from LPS, with details for this and the relevant search fees outlined on the website.

Museums
Belfast has many wonderful museums interpreting the various worlds of our ancestors, informing us of the historical context for the times within which they lived.

Ulster Museum
Botanic Gardens, Belfast, BT9 5AB
www.nmni.com

Founded in 1821 as the Belfast Natural History Society, the Ulster Museum today covers three main areas with its collections, on the themes of art, nature and history. The history section can provide an informative way to get to grips with the history of Ireland as a whole, but also aspects of Belfast's place within that. There are exhibits on ancient history as told from archaeological finds, such as the impressive Malone Hoard of nineteen polished Neolithic axe heads (found at Danesfort House on the Malone Road), the linen-weaving industry, and the recent Troubles.

Titanic Belfast / SS Nomadic
1 Olympic Way, Queen's Road, Titanic Quarter, Belfast, BT3 9EP
www.titanicbelfast.com
Tel: 028 9076 6386

The Titanic Belfast centre, located at the city docks, provides an interactive experience to visitors, exploring not just the construction of the RMS *Titanic* but also the wider story of the shipyards and those who worked

The Titanic Centre.

within them. (When it comes to the subsequent disaster that befell the ship, Belfast folk will always tell you that there was nothing wrong with her when she left!)

Close to the museum is the restored SS *Nomadic*, a former tender, which was used to transport passengers to the *Titanic*, which can also be visited. You can obtain a ticket for either attraction, or a combined ticket for both.

TIP: The Belfast Titanic Society was founded in 1992, and has a dedicated website at **www.belfast-titanic.com**. This site lists many suggested research resources, as well as some biographical information on individuals known to have worked for Harland and Wolff (p.144), and on the *Titanic*.

Northern Ireland War Memorial Museum
NI War Memorial, 21 Talbot Street, Belfast, BT1 2LD
www.niwarmemorial.org
Tel: 028 9032 0392
Email: info@niwarmemorial.org

This museum recalls the experiences of Belfast during the Second World War, not just with those who served in the armed forces but on the domestic front. It includes presentations on the strife suffered during the Belfast Blitz raids by the German Luftwaffe in 1941, the arrival of American GIs in the city, the role of the Ulster Home Guard, and the various manufacturing industries of the city during the conflict.

Royal Ulster Rifles Regimental Museum
2nd Floor, 28 Bedford Street, Belfast, BT7 2FE
www.royal-irish.com/museums/royal-ulster-rifles-museum
Tel: 028 9023 2086
Email: rurmuseum@yahoo.co.uk

This museum details the history of the Royal Ulster Rifles from its formation in 1793 (as the Royal Irish Rifles), and the subsequent campaigns within which it was involved, including the Boer War, the First and Second World Wars, and the Korean War.

Police Museum
Police Service of Northern Ireland Headquarters, Brooklyn, 65 Knock Road, Belfast, BT5 6LE
www.psni.police.uk/inside-psni/our-history/police-museum/
Email: museum@psni.police.uk

Located within a former sergeant's married quarters at the headquarters of the Police Service of Northern Ireland, the Police Museum provides an overview of the history of the Royal Irish Constabulary, and its successor service in Northern Ireland, the Royal Ulster Constabulary. The museum is also the base for the Police Historical Society.

The curator is able to provide access to copies of RIC service records from 1822 to 1922 (see **www.psni.police.uk/inside-psni/our-history/genealogy/**), although these can also be accessed via Findmypast (p.47).

HMS **Caroline**
Alexandra Dock, Queens Road, Belfast, BT3 9DT
www.nmrn.org.uk/visit-us/hms-caroline

HMS *Caroline* is a surviving Royal Navy vessel from the First World War, now based in the Titanic Quarter as a naval museum.

Museum of Orange Heritage
Schomberg House, 368 Cregagh Road, Belfast, BT6 9EY
www.orangeheritage.co.uk

If your ancestors were in the Orange Order, this museum can offer an insight into the organisation's history since its initial foundation in 1795 in County Armagh. The museum offers interpretations of events such as the Battle of the Boyne, the development of the Order, the Home Rule crisis, the First World War, and Partition, including details of how Orangeism has survived in the Republic since 1921, as well as its continuing existence in the north.

The museum's archive holds some lodge books, but not a lot of material from Belfast, with the majority of surviving books still held by local lodges. However, if you can supply details of the name of the member of interest and the relevant lodge number, and if the museum does not have relevant holdings, it will be happy to facilitate contact with the relevant lodge.

Further information about the society's holdings is described at **www. orangeheritage.co.uk/archives**.

The Museum of Orange Heritage, on Cregagh Road.

Eileen Hickey Irish Republican History Museum
5 Conway Place, Belfast, BT13 2DA
https://eileenhickeymuseum.com
Email: eileenhickeymuseum@yahoo.com
Tel: 028 9024 0504

A museum located in the Conway Mill Complex, just off the Falls Road, which is dedicated to portraying the Irish Republican perspective of the recent Troubles, and the wider history of Irish republicanism.

Ulster Transport Museum
153 Bangor Rd, Cultra, Holywood, BT18 0EU
www.ulstertransportmuseum.org
Tel: 028 9042 8428

The Transport Museum is just up the road from Belfast at Cultra in Co. Down, but is a great place to visit to see the vehicles of yesteryear as once used in the city. A guide to trams and buses in Belfast can be found on its website at **www.ulstertransportmuseum.org/stories/froms-trams-trolleybuses**.

> **TIP:** The Ulster Folk Museum is adjacent to the Transport Museum in Cultra, and is equally worth a visit. Find out more at **www. ulsterfolkmuseum.org**.

Chapter 4

ONLINE REPOSITORIES

Several popular commercial family history websites are available with a wealth of resources, which will occasionally be referenced in this book. Most will offer the option of a short trial subscription, and various subscription tiers should you wish to continue beyond that.

The following are the key sites that can help with Belfast-based research.

Ancestry
www.ancestry.co.uk
Ancestry is the UK's platform for the American-based Ancestry.com corporation. It has a dedicated Irish section accessible via **www.ancestry. co.uk/cs/irish**, but the most complete listings of Irish collections are to be found within the site's 'Card Catalogue', or by using the 'Explore by Location' map function on the main 'Search' page (Northern Ireland is listed under the 'United Kingdom' section).

The greatest strength of Ancestry for Belfast-based research probably lies within its many military collections, for the British Army, the Royal Navy, and the Royal Air Force, as sourced from the National Archives in England. There are well over 100 UK military collections, with the following amongst the most popularly used:

- UK, British Army World War I Service Records, 1914–1920
- UK, British Army World War I Pension Records, 1914–1920
- UK, World War I Pension Ledgers and Index Cards, 1914–1923
- UK, Royal Hospital Chelsea Pensioner Soldier Service Records, 1760–1920
- UK, Soldiers Died in the Great War, 1914–1919
- UK, Royal Air Force Operations Record Books, 1911–1963

- UK, World War II Allied Prisoners of War, 1939–1945
- UK, Navy Lists, 1888–1970
- UK, Naval Medal and Award Rolls, 1793–1972
- UK, Royal Navy Registers of Seamen's Services, 1848–1939

Beyond military research, the following collections can also be of use:

- Belfast, Northern Ireland, The Belfast Newsletter (Birth, Marriage and Death Notices), 1738–1925
- Ireland, Catholic Parish Registers, 1655–1915
- Ireland, Irish Emigration Lists, 1833–1839
- Ireland, Civil Registration Marriages Index, 1845–1958 *
- Ireland, Civil Registration Births Index, 1864–1958 *
- Ireland, Civil Registration Deaths Index, 1864–1958 *

* Note these are indexes only, and are only useful up to 1921 for Belfast enquiries – see p.67 for how to access the original records.

Ancestry also has some third-party index collections, which act as finding aids for collections held by other agencies. If an entry is of interest, Ancestry will then redirect you from its index to the site hosting the original record. Again, the following are useful for Belfast research:

- Web: Northern Ireland, Will Calendar Index, 1858–1965 (PRONI)
- Web: Belfast, Northern Ireland, Burial Indexes, 1869–2011 (Belfast City Council)
- Web: Ireland, Census, 1901 (NAI) *
- Web: Ireland, Census, 1911 (NAI) *

* Note that Ancestry's versions of the 1901 and 1911 censuses allow for you to search for more than one individual in a household at a time, unlike the NAI's own platform (p.92).

One other majorly useful offering on Ancestry is its autosomal DNA-testing facility (p.172). The site allows you to upload a family tree to its platform via a basic free-to-access subscription, and will allow you to see if the site has any records matches for individuals named on the tree (although you will need a paid subscription to be able to view these). This tree can be made private or public for others to search.

If you subsequently do a DNA test, and link the results to your tree, it is possible for distant cousins who have also tested to potentially make a connection with you, with common ancestors on their trees matching relatives on yours.

For more on the use of DNA testing in family history research, consult my book *Sharing Your Family History Online* (Pen and Sword 2021).

Findmypast
www.findmypast.co.uk / www.findmypast.ie
Findmypast is a similar subscription-based site with various Irish record sets, and additional UK materials. These wider collections include the following useful databases for Belfast research:

- British Army Service Records
- British Army, Irish Regimental Enlistment Registers, 1877–1924
- British Armed Forces, First World War Soldiers' Medical Records
- British Army, Worldwide Index, 1841
- British Army, Worldwide Index, 1851
- British Army, Worldwide Index, 1861
- British Army, Worldwide Index, 1871
- British Royal Navy & Royal Marines Service and Pension Records, 1704–1919
- British Civil Service Evidence Of Age
- Ireland, Northern Ireland Deaths, 1998–2020
- Ireland Census, 1901 *
- Ireland Census, 1911 *

* As with Ancestry, Findmypast permits searches of the Irish 1901 and 1911 censuses with more than one individual in a household at a time.

Again, a full search of this site's catalogue, accessible via the 'Search' menu option at the top of the page, and then 'All Record Sets', will yield many more possibilities.

Findmypast also has some very specific holdings for the city:

- Ireland, Belfast & Ulster Directories *(covering 1890–1948)*
- Ireland, Belfast Gazette, 1922–2018
- Henderson's Belfast Directory, 1850
- Matier's Belfast Directory for 1835–6

One area where Findmypast more than holds its own against Ancestry is with its 'Irish Newspapers' collection, which reproduces the same digitised newspaper titles from the British Newspaper Archive (p.48), but within the site's wider 'Pro' subscription. Whilst this can save the need for a separate subscription to its partner site, Findmypast's search screen for its newspaper holdings is not quite as intuitive.

Findmypast also permits you to sign up for a basic free subscription which allows you to host your family tree. This will flag up any record matches that the site may have for individuals mentioned, but you will need a paid subscription, or pay-per-view credits, to be able to view them.

> **TIP:** You can get free two-week trial periods for both Ancestry and Findmypast, but once you have signed up, cancel your subscription, you will still get the free two-week period. If you don't cancel before the end of the trial period, your account will be renewed and you may be charged.

MyHeritage
www.myheritage.com
Although it does not offer a great deal for Ireland, MyHeritage does offer some gems, such as an Irish Jewish database (p.77), and a searchable version of the Irish censuses (p.91) that allow you to search by more than one person at a time in a household.

> **TIP:** Ancestry, Findmypast, MyHeritage and TheGenealogist (www. thegenealogist.co.uk) are four of the key sites to help you look for Belfast emigrants within England and Wales, and internationally. For Scotland, visit the pay-per-view-based ScotlandsPeople platform at **www.scotlandpeople.gov.uk**.

British Newspaper Archive
www.britishnewspaperarchive.co.uk
The British Newspaper Archive (BNA) is a collaboration between the British Library and Findmypast, which hosts millions of pages of searchable digitised newspaper content from across Britain and Ireland.

A subscription website, its offerings include the following:

- *Belfast Telegraph*
- *Belfast Newsletter*
- *Belfast Commercial Chronicle*
- *Belfast Mercantile Register and Weekly Advertiser*
- *Belfast Mercury*

- *Belfast Morning News*
- *Belfast Protestant Journal*
- *Belfast Weekly News*
- *Belfast Weekly Telegraph*
- *Ireland's Saturday Night*

In addition are many additional national titles published in Dublin prior to Partition.

> **TIP:** The same records are available through a Findmypast Pro subscription (see above), however, if choosing to access this way, be advised that the search interface on the British Newspaper Archive website is much superior to that on Findmypast – so perhaps use this to carry out your free searches initially, and then access the images for the records found through your Findmypast subscription.

Irish Newspaper Archives
www.irishnewsarchive.com
The Irish Newspaper Archives is another major player for Irish newspaper research, a subscription platform which includes the *Belfast Newsletter* and the *Belfast Telegraph*, as well as several other northern and all-Ireland-based titles.

Also included is the 'Radical Irish Newspaper Archive', dealing with the politics and events of the revolutionary period in Ireland, featuring 115 newspaper titles covering the War of Independence and the Civil War, as well as the politics of their immediate aftermath.

Eddie's Extracts
www.eddiesextracts.com
Eddie Connolly should be saluted also for this incredible effort, a free-to-access database which contains many newspaper intimations for births, marriages and deaths, as well as stories and announcements. These have been drawn from titles such as the *Belfast Telegraph*, *The Witness*, *The Banner of Ulster*, the *Northern Whig*, the *Lisburn Standard*, with the earliest entries being from the *Belfast Commercial Chronicle* in February 1805.

As well as the newspaper extracts, Eddie has also made available Presbyterian Rolls of Honour from the two world wars, the Soldiers Died in the Great War database, Church of Ireland rolls of honour from congregations in Belfast (such as St Michael's and St Matthew's), and a roll for the Civil Defence Service of the Belfast Blitz from 1941.

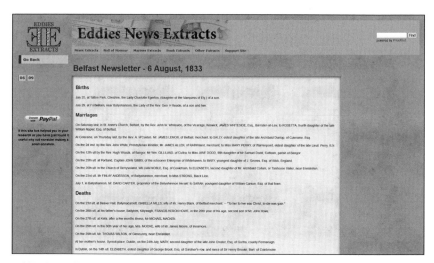

Eddie Connolly's excellent Eddie's Extracts platform.

In addition are the histories of several Belfast churches, such as First Presbyterian, the Second Congregation of Dissenters, St Aidan's Church of Ireland, St Mark's (Dundela) Church of Ireland, and St Paul's Church of Ireland (York Street).

FamilySearch
www.familysearch.org

FamilySearch is the online platform of the Church of Jesus Christ of Latter-day Saints (p.33). The site offers some records to users for free, although, as mentioned previously, church members can gain access to many additional resources that are blocked from access to the general public due to licensing issues. These closed records, however, can be viewed by the general public at a family history centre, including at its Belfast Family History Centre. FamilySearch has a large research library in Salt Lake City, Utah, with its holdings detailed on the catalogue.

There are several useful tools on the FamilySearch platform for Belfast-based research. These include its catalogue, located under the Search menu options at the top of the page, through which you can freely access

TIP: FamilySearch has been challenged for a while when it comes to categorising materials for Northern Ireland, so you will find most useful resources for Belfast under the 'Ireland' category, rather than 'Northern Ireland', or within the 'England' category, as part of several 'Great Britain' or 'UK' collections!

collections such as the Irish Registry of Deeds (p.112), and the digitised records available through its 'Search Historical Records by Place' section at **www.familysearch.org/search/location/list**.

RootsIreland
www.rootsireland.ie
The online platform for the Irish Family History Foundation, this subscription-based resource offers transcribed records from a variety of sources, including civil- and church-based vital register records. The records for Belfast are split between Counties Antrim and Down, and are sourced from the Ulster Historical Foundation (p.31).

Emerald Ancestors
www.emeraldancestors.com
A further subscription-based platform offering access to indexed vital records. Amongst its other holdings is a transcribed 1852 Church of Ireland census for Christchurch, Belfast, and indexed records for Campbell College (see p.121).

The Belfast History Project
www.belfasthistoryproject.com
This site, created by the Glenravel Local History Project, now the Belfast History Project), offers a detailed timeline of the city from the 1830s to 1941, as well as downloadable books of photos of Belfast from 1920 to the 1960s, searchable guides to Clifton Street Cemetery, and copies of its wonderful *Old Belfast* magazine.

Discussion Forums
There are plenty of folk out there with expertise to help with your brick wall issues, who can assist via discussion forums, where you can post a query and brainstorm an issue between you! The following are perhaps the best for Belfast-based research:

Belfast Forum
www.belfastforum.co.uk
A dedicated online discussion forum for all things Belfast founded in 2006, the site is still going strong, with sections on the site, including 'Belfast Genealogy', 'Belfast History and Memories', 'Old Belfast Photos', and 'Exiles'.

Rootschat

www.rootschat.com

RootsChat is the best-known family history discussion forum across the UK and Ireland, with well over 6 million posts and over a quarter of a million users. Within the site there are dedicated sections covering a variety of topics, including the armed forces, DNA testing, the individual countries of the UK and Ireland (Northern Ireland and the Republic of Ireland are covered in a single board), and elsewhere around the world. Access is free, requiring a simple registration.

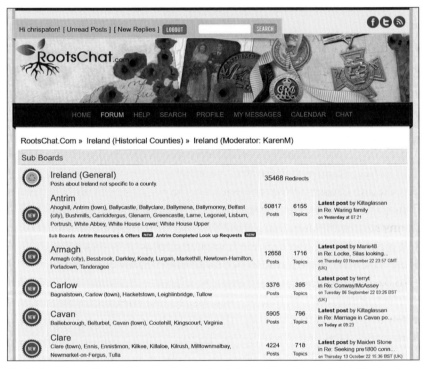

RootsChat has a substantial community of family historians who can help with enquiries.

The Great War Forum

www.greatwarforum.org

On military matters, the Great War Forum covers just about every topic that you may wish to discuss for the First World War, with many military historians only too happy to assist with enquiries.

> **TIP:** Ancestry has an archive of its Message Boards, which are also worth exploring for posts from the last two decades – you'll find these under the Help menu option.

Chapter 5

FROM THE CRADLE
TO THE GRAVE

If you are starting to research your family history for the first time, begin by establishing what you do or do not know about your family, and then work out how to fill in the gaps. If you grew up in Belfast yourself, or knew family from the city, first write down what you can remember about them. Who were your parents, grandparents, aunts and uncles, and cousins? What religious denominations did family members adhere to? Who went to school where? What jobs did they have, what funny stories are often told about them that you know of, and what were the moments of crisis? Once you have done this, you will have a rough idea about the most recent chapters of your family story, but you will also be able to identify some key gaps in your knowledge.

If you have relatives that you can discuss the family story with, invite them to talk to you, and ask if they can help to flesh out the picture a little more. Some may be only too happy to do so, perhaps equally as curious as yourself. At the other end of the scale, you may also come across relatives responding with a traditional 'Och, sure, what do you want to know that for?', and refusing to engage. Family history research can be a rewarding but invasive process, and people have a right to privacy, so don't fall out with them over it. It may be that in time, as you begin to make discoveries about your ancestry, that some of your more reticent relatives may begin to show an interest, but there is no obligation for them to do so, and they may well have some very deep and personal reasons for simply not wishing to know. Always respect that – this should be your hobby, and not their ordeal.

At this initial stage you will have a rough idea of what you think the start of the family story is, but there is a caveat. What you have before

The author's grandmother, Jean Paton (née. Currie), in her garden at Whitewell Crescent in 1938.

you may be accurate, but it equally may not. People's memories can be funny things, particularly with older relatives; events may have been confused, names mixed up, and vague half-stories recollected which may not turn out to be true. The next step, therefore, is to try to prove everything that you have remembered and have been told, working from known, confirmed events, one stage at a time, back towards the unknown.

TIP: Be very careful about what you may find online on certain family history websites hosting family trees. It can be very tempting to jump on to a site, and within minutes find a page that purports to show your ancestry going back to William the Conqueror, Robert the Bruce, or Brian Boru. However, the information presented may be utter nonsense. Where such trees are dutifully presented with source information, perhaps including copies of original documents, you will truly have found the goose with the golden egg. But if no sources are displayed, trust any information presented as far as you can throw it, until you have corroborated the details for yourself.

Civil registration

The first records that you will need to get to grips with are those produced by the civil registration systems in Ireland. When registration was first established from April 1845, it was for the purpose of registering non-Roman Catholic marriages only, i.e. marriages in the Protestant-denominated churches, as well as civil marriages performed by registrars, which could be performed for people from all faiths. The Roman Catholic Church at this stage declined to participate, viewing the requirements of the state to be an unwanted intrusion into a religious event.

To administer the new system, the country was divided into a series of Registration Districts (RDs) based on the Poor Law Unions that had been established in 1838 to handle the provisions of the reformed poor law (see p.126). Belfast was constituted as one of these districts, and administered by William McComb, the area's first registrar for marriages, who regularly transmitted copies of his records to the Registrar General in Dublin, where they were then indexed at the General Register Office.

From January 1864, the law was expanded to facilitate the registration of all births, marriages (irrespective of denomination) and deaths. The registrar of Protestant and civil marriages for each RD, including Belfast, was now styled as its 'superintendent registrar', with each district also re-designated as a 'Superintendent Registrar's District' (SRD).

At the same time, new localised posts of registrars of births, deaths and Roman Catholic marriages were set up to oversee the wider system, which used the smaller administrative boundaries of medical dispensary districts as convenient subdivisions of the Poor Law Union. In most cases, existent medical officers of health were employed as registrars to record births, deaths and Roman Catholic marriages, whose work was overseen in turn by their respective superintendent registrar, who continued to register non-Roman Catholic marriages. In Belfast, the following were the dispensary districts that formed the earliest registration districts within the city:

- Ballygomartin
- Ballymacarrett
- Barrack Street, Belfast, and Lancaster Street, Belfast
- Carnmoney
- Holywood
- Whitehouse

The subsequent evolution of the Registrar Districts from 1880 is outlined on p.18.

Registration of births, marriages, civil partnerships and deaths is today carried out at Belfast City Hall.

In 1922, following Partition, Belfast was chosen to become the base of a new General Register Office for Northern Ireland (GRONI), initially located on Royal Avenue, with copies of historical birth and death registers transmitted north from Dublin to the new agency. In its earliest years GRONI moved its location frequently, being based in various government offices at Donegall Square West, Murray Street, May Street, Ormeau Road (Fermanagh House), and College Street.

Registration continued on the same basis as before, with returns from the city registrars sent to the new Northern Irish Registrar General on a weekly basis, where they would in turn be indexed on an annual basis, and with statistical reports collated on a regular basis.

A major change in 1973 saw Northern Ireland's twenty-six district councils, of which Belfast formed one, taking over responsibility for registration, with the superintendent registrar in each area now replaced by a Registrar of Births, Marriages and Deaths, aided by deputy registrars. From this point, sub-districts were no longer in use. The registration system continues to evolve, with one of the most recent changes introduced in March 2022 being the option to register vital records events in the Irish language rather than in English, or bilingually in both languages.

The records of civil registration, which are today compiled by the registration services of the General Register Office for Northern Ireland (p.23), will almost certainly be the most important that you will need to use and understand as you travel back with your research to the mid-nineteenth century. I will now look at each record type in turn to show what they might contain, and to illustrate how they may help you to build your family tree.

Births

The following is a typical example of a birth record from Belfast, in this case for William Graham, a younger brother to my two times great-grandfather Edwin Graham. William was born in 1864, the first year of registration:

No.	Date and Place of Birth	Name (if any)	Sex	Name and Surname and Dwelling Place of Father	Name and Surname and Maiden Surname of Mother	Rank or Profession of Father	Signature, Qualification and Residence of Informant	When Registered	Signature of Registrar	Baptismal Name, if added after Registration of Birth, and Date
338	Eighteenth November 1864, 86 Henry Street, Belfast	William	Male	Thomas Graham, 86 Henry Street	Eliza Graham formerly Taylor	Son of a Millworker	Eliza Graham (her X mark), Mother, 86 Henry Street	Second December 1864	Echlin Gordon, Deputy Registrar	

As can be seen, the record shows William's first name and surname, the names of both of his parents, where and when he was born, the details of his father's occupation and residence (which may not necessarily be where the child was born), and details of the informant, in this case William's mother, Eliza. The note stating 'her X mark' means that Eliza was illiterate, and had to sign with a simple cross.

This is a record for a 'legitimate' birth, i.e. one where the child's parents were married prior to its birth, but it is worth noting that the initial 1863 Act for the Registration of Births and Deaths in Ireland did not state how 'illegitimate' children, i.e. children born to unmarried parents, should be recorded. It was not until a revising act of 1874 was passed that registrars were instructed not to note the name of an illegitimate child's father 'unless at the joint request of the mother and of the person acknowledging himself to be the father of such child'. In such circumstances, both the mother and the father had to attend the registry office and sign the register together.

In 1928, the Legitimacy Act (Northern Ireland) would later permit a child to be retrospectively legitimised if their parents subsequently married, so long as they had been free to marry when the child was conceived, i.e. that the child was not born from an adulterous relationship. For earlier births, the name of the father may be omitted from the civil record, but it may be yet noted in a subsequent baptismal record (p.67). If a child's birth cannot be found, it may be because it is indexed under the mother's maiden name, rather than the father's surname.

In the earliest period of registration, the child's forename did not have to be included in the record, which may not have been decided on prior to its baptism. Indeed, in the example of William's younger sister Wilhelmina, born on 2 February 1871, this was the case, with her forename left blank in her birth record. As can be seen from the last column, it was possible to have the forename added later to the record after baptism, which did not necessarily happen.

Marriages

Knowing the name of a child's parents allows you to move back a bit further, to try to find their marriage record. From April 1845, it was possible to register non-Roman Catholic marriages, including civil marriages, in Belfast, but from January 1864 all marriages were registered by the state, including those performed in Roman Catholic churches. For religious marriages there is some minor variation in the records depending on the type of ceremony involved, as each of the churches became the de facto registrar for marriages on their patch.

Let's consider two examples. The first record is for my two times great-grandfather Edwin's second marriage in 1912, at Fortwilliam Presbyterian Church:

1912 Marriage solemnized at Fortwilliam Park Church in the parish of Shankill in the Co. of Antrim									
No.	When married	Name and Surname	Age	Condition	Rank or Profession	Residence at the Time of Marriage	Fathers Name and Surname	Rank or Profession of Father
55	September 30th	Edwin Graham	Full	Widower	Riviter [sic]	Belfast	Thomas Graham	Deceased
		Matilda Blair	Full	Spinster	-	Belfast	John Blair	Deceased
Married in the Church according to the Form and Discipline of the Presbyterian Church, by license, by me, Thomas M. Johnstone									
This Marriage was solemnized between us	Edwin Graham		In the presence of us		Charles Richardson			
	Matilda Blair				Sarah Richardson			

This second example is for the marriage in 1888 of a John McLea and Jane Campbell at St Patrick's Roman Catholic Chapel (Donegall Street):

No.	When married	Name and Surname	Age	Condition	Rank or Profession	Residence at the Time of Marriage	Fathers Name and Surname	Rank or Profession of Father
86	16th April 1888	John McLea	23	Bachelor	Vandriver	58 Spamount St	Edward Carberry alive	Carter
		Jane Campbell	19	Spinster	Teacher	99 New Lodge Road	John Campbell alive	Carter

1888 marriage solemnized at the Roman Catholic Chapel of St Patrick in the Registrar's District of Belfast No. 2 in the Union of Belfast in the County of Antrim.

Married in the Roman Catholic Chapel of St Patrick's according to the Rites and Ceremonies of the Roman Catholic Church by me, John McDonnell C.C.

This Marriage was solemnized between us	Edward Carberry	In the presence of us	John McDade
	Jane Campbell		Mary Magill

You can see that how some of the information presented can be occasionally vague. Whilst spouses' correct ages are sometimes noted, as in the second example, you will often see ages listed as presented in the first, with both simply listed as 'Full', meaning that they were 21 or above, known as the 'age of majority'. It was in fact legally possible until 1951 to get married in Northern Ireland as young as 12, if you were a girl, and 14, if a boy; in such cases, the age description is often noted as 'Minor', although in the second example here we can see that Jane Campbell was aged 19. From 1 January 1970, the age of majority changed in Northern Ireland to 18, but it has remained possible to marry as young as 16 with parental permission (at the time of writing a consultation is underway about the possibility of raising this to 18).

Below the details of the contracting parties, the records note the celebrants carrying out the marriage, and by what means. In the first example, the marriage was performed according to the forms and discipline of the Presbyterian Church 'by licence', a common find in such records. Following the 1844 Registration Act, marriages could be performed following the purchase of a licence, or after the calling of banns on three successive Sundays before a relevant congregation, with processes in place for the registration of objections, or for the discoveries of irregularities to prevent a marriage taking place. For various historical reasons, the Presbyterian, Church of Ireland and Roman Catholic communities were more inclined towards the use of licences, rather than the publishing of banns, but towards the late nineteenth century the Catholic Church began to favour the use of banns due to changes within its own canon laws. In the second example, the Catholic ceremony is performed by a John McDonnell – the 'C.C.' after his name stands for 'Catholic Curate'; you will also see 'P.P.' in other records, meaning 'Parish Priest'.

The records also give the names of the spouses' fathers, but not their mothers. Under 'Rank or Profession' the fathers' occupations will be usually listed also, although in the first case it is simply stated that both are deceased. Something to be aware of is that if a record does not note that a father is deceased, this may not necessarily mean that he is alive. In the second example there is no dubiety, with both fathers specifically stated to be alive, and their occupations also noted.

Two witnesses were also required to be in attendance at a ceremony, whether religious or civil. It may not be clear who these were, but family members were often called upon to do the job.

> **TIP:** You may find that the names of female witnesses are sisters, aunts or cousins, listed under their married surnames, whilst males may be in-laws, which can be a useful clue to help flesh out the family further.

The key details to help you trace further back in your tree are the two spouses' names and ages, and their fathers' names. Unfortunately, mothers' names are not included, which can be awkward if the father has a common name, such as 'John Smyth', the name of my three times great-grandfather, believed to have come from Springfield village.

Occasionally, in more rural parts you may find that the spouses' addresses are simply given as townlands, e.g. 'Greencastle'. In the more urbanised parts of the city though, you will usually get a street address, but occasionally you might simply find the address unhelpfully noted as just 'Belfast'.

Deaths

Death records tend to be the easiest to find, as a death certificate was required for a burial and to claim a potential life insurance policy, if there was one. However, they unfortunately provide the least amount of information.

In this example, we can see information presented in the death record for my two times great-grandfather Thomas Smith, who died in the city in 1914:

No.	Date and Place of Death	Name and Surname	Sex	Condition	Age last Birthday	Rank, Profession or Occupation	Certified Cause of Death and Duration of Illness	Signature, Qualification and Residence of Informant	When Registered	Signature of Registrar
429	1914 Twenty Eighth November 51 Lisburn Road	Thomas Smith from 33 Bann St	M	Widower	56 years	Bleacher	Valvular Disease of Heart cardiac failure certified	J. Mahood Occupier 51 Lisburn Road	Thirtieth November 1914	A. Morrison, Asst. Registrar

The first point to note here is that although given as Smith in this record, the family surname in more recent generations of my family has been styled as Smyth (as in his father, John Smyth, mentioned earlier) – you may need to look for variants of a name if it cannot be found under the expected spelling.

Thomas is stated to have died at 51 Lisburn Road, but as being 'from 33 Bann Street', which was his residential address at the time. The informant, J. Mahood, was also listed as being the occupier of 51 Lisburn Road. However, in looking at this record on Irishgenealogy.ie (p.62), we can see from the same page of the register that J. Mahood was also the informant for three other deaths in the same month, and that they all died at the same address. The reason, which is not at all obvious from the record, is that 51 Lisburn Road was in fact the Belfast Union Infirmary, initially established as part of the city's workhouse. It is always worth checking out an unfamiliar address.

> **TIP:** If not a hospital, an unusual address may be that of another family member looking after a relative in their illness.

Thomas is also noted to be a widower, but there is no information about his former wife. You will rarely see the name of a wife unless she is the person who has died, or is the informant for her husband's registration; conversely, you will sometimes see the name of a woman's husband on her own death record, where her 'rank, profession or occupation' may state that she was the wife or widow of a particular person. Where a child has died, you may find the name of a parent specifically listed as the mother or father, if he or she was the informant.

The 'age last birthday' information can also be extremely helpful. If the marriage record for a person stated their age to be simply 'full' or 'minor', the age on the death record may provide the extra clue to take you back to try to find a birth record in the right period. But a key caveat needs to be pointed out here on this, and indeed all information provided in the record: the deceased was not the informant, and so information provided may be what the informant believed to be correct, but not necessarily what was correct. Stated ages can often be out by a few years in earlier records.

From 1973, death records have also included the original date and place of birth of the deceased, but again bear in mind that this information is only as accurate as the informant offering the details. For example, having spent many years in Belfast, my grandfather, Charles Paton, ended his days at a care home in Donaghadee in September 1987. In his death record, my aunt had informed the registrar that he had been born in Inverness, Scotland, in 1904; in fact, he had been born in Brussels, Belgium, a year later, to two Scottish parents. Question everything!

> **TIP:** It is important to 'kill off' an ancestor, so that you do not pursue someone else with the same name, thinking it to be the same person, when they may have already passed away.

Accessing civil registration records

A substantial number of historical civil registration records can be accessed online, but for more recent generations, you will run into problems. Birth records within the last 100 years, marriage records from the last seventy-five, and death records from the last fifty, are not online (to protect the privacy of those still living), but these can be accessed at both GRONI (p.23) and PRONI (p.24). If you have family members willing to let you have copies of records that they may hold, this may save you a bit of money, but do bear in mind the privacy concerns of those mentioned within them who may still be alive.

The good news is that virtually all of the earliest civil registration records from 1845 to 1921 for Belfast (and all of Northern Ireland) are freely available online at **www.irishgenealogy.ie** under the 'Civil Records' menu option (also directly via **https://civilrecords.irishgenealogy.ie**), as part of a platform administered on behalf of the Republic of Ireland's Department of Tourism, Culture, Arts, Gaeltacht and Sports.

Upon arrival at the search page, you will be asked to type in the following:

• First Name and Last Name of the person being sought – the site is not great for searching for surname variants, so you may need to try alternative spellings

- Civil Registration District/Office – in this case, you can only use 'Belfast' as a search term, and not the more localised registrars' districts
- Year Range – bear in mind that if an event occurred late in a year, it may not have been registered until the start of the next
- The type of record – Birth, Marriage or Death (select which is required)

There is a more advanced search screen available also, but often the basic search screen will suffice.

Once you click 'Search' you will be asked to tick a box stating that you are not a robot, and after answering a quick question on a subsequent page to prove it, you will be asked to input your name and to tick the box to acknowledge that 'you are making an application to search the indexes in line with the legislation outlined above' (i.e. Section 61 of the Republic's Civil Registration Act, 2004). You can now click on 'Submit', and the list of possible record entries will be returned for you.

Results are presented to the right side of the search returns page, noting basic details such as a person's name, a 'Group Registration ID' number, and the district in question. Clicking on an entry takes you to a new page with basic index details, and a link to the image. Options to report transcription errors and page problems are also available. Once you click on the link, a downloadable PDF image of the page from the register will open, which will usually contain more than one entry. You can download and save this page to your computer.

> **TIP:** If you are unable to find a child in a search, try again by searching with the surname only, in case the child had yet to be formally baptised.
>
> It may be that the event was not registered, something more commonly found in the earlier period of registration. In such cases, parish records may still be of some assistance, providing evidence of the child's baptisms, and which may possibly also note the date of birth.

For records following Partition in 1921, as compiled by GRONI, you need to visit its website instead at **https://geni.nidirect.gov.uk**. The first key difference with this site is that it offers the records on a pay-per-view basis only.

On this site there are four separate search screens, for birth registrations, marriages, deaths, and 'WWII registration' (overseas military deaths from the Second World War involving Northern Irish personnel). Each screen offers the following search terms:

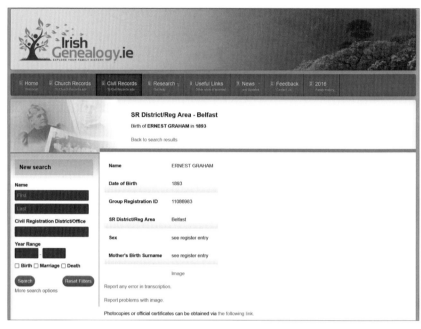

The IrishGenealogy.ie platform offers free access to pre-1922 records for Belfast.

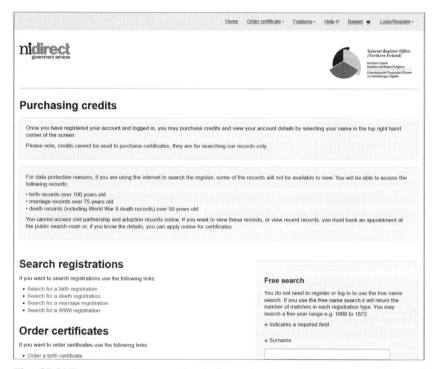

The GRONI's pay-per-view records platform also hosts historical records beyond Partition.

- Surname of child, forename of child, and mother's maiden name – you can use the small drop-down menus to the right of each search field to specify 'equals' (for an exact spelling), 'Begins with' (the first few letters in a name), or 'Variants' (for possible spelling variations).
- Sex of child – male, female, or undetermined/unknown
- Date of birth (or marriage or death) – if you have it
- Year or year range – this only allows you to search in groups of five years at a time, e.g. 1923–1927. If you know the exact year, type this into the first box only. Again, remember that an event that occurred at the end of one year may not have been formally registered until the start of the next.
- Registration district pre-1973 – select 'Belfast'
- Registration sub-district – this is also for the pre-1973 period. For Belfast, you have various options: Belfast No.1–3, Belfast Urban 1–21, Belfast Rural 1–4, and Castlereagh No. 1–3

> **TIP:** Have at least one credit on your account, as this will help to unlock some very limited free information when carrying out searches.

The amount of free information from a basic search is surprisingly detailed.

- Births: a registration number, the child's first name and surname, the date of birth, the mother's maiden name and the registration district.
- Marriages: the name of a candidate, the surname of the spouse, the wedding date and the registration district
- Deaths: name, age at death, date of death, and the registration district.

After carrying out a basic search, a fuller, although not complete, transcript of additional information can be obtained at a cost of one credit, by clicking the 'Enhanced' link to the right of the search result. To see the original image itself, with all of the relevant information, will cost five credits, obtained by clicking the 'Full' option beside the index entry. On viewing the latter, the transcript is displayed beneath an image of the original record.

Despite this being a pay-per-view site, there is a possible advantage to using the GRONI site over IrishGenealogy.ie for the periods where the same records are hosted. The records held and digitised by the GRONI are from the primary registers, whilst the records held at the Irish GRO in

Dublin are duplicates. You will easily see this when consulting the same record on both sites, where they will appear in different handwriting – something to consider if one site's version proves hard to read!

Because IrishGenealogy.ie hosts copies, errors occasionally crop up. If we look at the example on page 58 concerning Edwin Graham's second marriage to Matilda Blair in 1912, his condition is noted as a 'widower', with his first wife Florence having passed away in the city a year before. This is the record sourced from the GRONI site. However, the same record on IrishGenealogy.ie notes Edwin's condition as a 'bachelor'. If I had only used this site, I may never have known of his earlier marriage.

> **TIP:** Free records are not necessarily better. Keep an open mind!

Beyond the closure periods, there are unfortunately no indexes presented online for more recent records. However, GRONI does offer three alternative means to obtain copies of such records:

- If you live beyond Belfast you can apply for a certified record copy using the GRONI website at **https://geni.nidirect.gov.uk** – simply scroll down to the section marked 'Order certificates' to make your application. You will be charged considerably more for a certified copy; at the time of writing the cost is £15 for a full certificate (£8 for the document, plus a £7 search fee). Adoption register records and more recent civil partnership records can also be purchased, and you can pay for all records online by credit or debit card.
- Alternatively, if you live in Belfast or can get to the city, you can book a visit to the GRONI's public search room at Colby Court to search the records, using your same account (see p.23). Although the historical records presented online have closure periods, there are no such barriers to accessing more recent records in the search rooms. Any register images purchased, however, cannot be viewed on your account when you return home, and thus you will need to transcribe all the relevant details whilst you are there.
- If you are planning to visit PRONI at Titanic Quarter, you will also find a small number of terminals in its Search Room that offer access to the GRONI website's more recent records. Note that the PRONI staff cannot assist with any problems concerning the site; for example, if you forget your password, you may end up having to call GRONI to ask it to change it for you. You also cannot book a seat at PRONI – if

there is a lot of demand for the terminals you may be asked to limit your time on them to allow others a chance to gain access also.

The Church of Jesus Christ of Latter-day Saints (p.33) has microfilmed some early registers of births, marriages and death certificates. For a guide to what was imaged visit **www.nidirect.gov.uk/sites/default/files/ publications/Civil-registers-and-indexes-of-births-marriages-deaths. pdf**.

There are no GRONI indexes available online for births, marriages and deaths online after 1922, but one resource that might help is a database on Ancestry (p.45) entitled 'Scotland and Northern Ireland, Death Index, 1989–2020'. The source of this, GreyPower Deceased Data, as compiled by Wilmington Millennium in West Yorkshire, is believed to be from insurance policies, and carries basic details of about 45 per cent of those listed as having passed away in Northern Ireland, such as their name, date of death and place of death, which may help.

A similar collection is found in Findmypast's 'Ireland, Northern Ireland Deaths 1998–2020' collection.

> **TIP:** Other types of records can be obtained from GRONI as certified extracts. For adoption certificates from 1931 onwards visit **www. nidirect.gov.uk/services/order-adoption-certificate-online**. For civil partnership certificates from 2005 visit **www.nidirect.gov.uk/ services/order-civil-partnership-certificate-online**.

Church records
Prior to the records of civil registration, the records to go to for earlier information about births/baptisms, marriages and deaths/burials in Belfast are the parish registers from the city's many church denominations. In the appendix to the *Royal Irish Academy's Irish Historic Towns Atlas No.17*, which covers Belfast from 1840 to 1900, there is a listing within this period of twenty-two Church of Ireland congregations, sixty-three Presbyterian congregations (from different denominations), ten Roman Catholic chapels, thirty-four Methodist meetings (of various flavours), and seven Baptist churches, not to mention convents, Evangelical Union congregations, mission halls, Salvation Army barracks, independent churches, and more. Congregations formed, occasionally moved, and sometimes closed, and thus tracking down where your ancestors actually worshipped across time can become quite a task.

Whilst there is no one-stop shop online to locate copies of records, there are certainly useful resources to help indicate whether records that you might wish to see for an area actually exist in the first place. The PRONI website hosts two substantial documents entitled *Guide to Church Records* and *Church Records Available as Digital Copies in PRONI*.

The first of these is by far the more substantial, and essentially lists in alphabetical order by place the names of all churches, congregations and classes that PRONI is aware of, outlining the years for which records are known to exist, the information required to consult them if on site (microfilm numbers, call numbers for original documents), where surviving material is held that is not at PRONI itself, and whether records that are absent are known not to have survived. The information presented for Belfast's churches is some eighteen pages in length.

Church of Ireland

The state church in Ireland until 1871 was the Church of Ireland, an Anglican-based sister denomination to the Church of England. It is sometimes referred to as the 'Episcopal Church', due to the fact that it has an episcopal hierarchy, with bishops and archbishops (as with the Roman Catholic Church). Although Belfast spent much of its existence dominated by Presbyterian congregations, thanks to the influx of Scottish

The Church of Ireland's St Anne's Cathedral first opened in the city in 1904.

settlers, the Church of Ireland was also present from the outset of the city's foundation as a charter town.

PRONI has a substantial collection of records for the denomination, with the *Guide to Church Records* identifying holdings for some twenty-three churches, and identifies others 'in local custody', i.e. still with the church. Some of the records are original holdings deposited with the archive, whilst others are microfilms, and in more recent years, digitised copies.

A good example is if I look for records that might help with ancestors who belonged to the Church of Ireland congregation at St Anne's, parish of Shankill. The PRONI document informs me that there are baptismal records available on microfilm from 1745 to 1901, marriages from 1745 to 1900, and burials from 1745 to 1809, 1824 to 65, 1878 and 1883. That sounds great, but there is a particular problem with the microfilms, parts of which are completely illegible due to poor production methods when they were first created. However, the section on St Anne's also tells me that the original volumes are held at PRONI, and just for good measure, that they are also available as digital records, having recently been scanned again by the archive from the original volumes.

These digital records are not online, and can only be consulted in the PRONI Search Room in Belfast, but the quality far surpasses those found on the microfilms. In addition, the coverage is slightly extended on these, with baptisms up to 1911, and marriages up to 1914. The entry for St Anne's also tells me that more recent burial records from 1884 onwards are 'in local custody', and that there is a printed volume of transcripts from the marriage register covering the period 1745–1799.

TIP: Some St Anne's baptisms from 1764 to 1771 are found transcribed in Ulster Ancestry's County Antrim section at **www.ulsterancestry. com**.

By contrast, the coverage news is not so good for the Church of Ireland congregation at St Matthew's. The microfilm for baptisms covers 1846–1893, and for marriages 1856–1897. On the digital records, the availability of baptisms is extended up to 1905, and marriages up to 1916, whilst there are also burial records from 1887 to 1917.

But what about before this? Unfortunately, the entry notes 'Earliest records destroyed in Dublin'. This refers to the opening act of the Irish Civil War, when a wing of the Irish Republican Army, which did not agree with the Anglo-Irish Treaty of 1921, broke away to resist their former colleagues who had voted to agree its ratification at the Dáil, the Irish parliament. The dissenters, known as the 'Irregulars', captured the Four Courts complex in Dublin in 1922, which contained the Public Record Office of Ireland, and refused to surrender. In the bombardment that subsequently followed, an explosion of munitions on the site utterly levelled the facility, and as a consequence, a substantial number of Ireland's historical records were destroyed. This included many Church of Ireland parish records, they having been deposited there from 1871 onwards, following the body's disestablishment as the state church. Fortunately, a great deal of Belfast's records did survive, or at least in some cases, copies of them did, but you will find gaps – the entry for St Paul's (Connor diocese), for example, simply notes all the earliest registers to have been similarly destroyed, with nothing available to consult.

It is also worth noting that the following records from Belfast are held in Dublin at the Representative Church Body Library (**www.ireland. anglican.org/about/rcb-library**):

- Holy Redeemer (baptisms 1968–1992)
- Mount Merrion, Church of the Pentecost (marriages 1962–1994)
- St James (baptisms and marriages 1878–2008, and burials 1867–1870)
- St Mary (baptisms 1867–1957, marriages 1869–1988, burials 1867–1870)
- St Peter (baptisms 1896–2006, marriages 1901–1999)
- St Peter, Chapel of the Resurrection (marriages 1941–1972)
- TCD Mission (baptisms 1938–1962, marriages 1947–1968)

Detailed catalogue entries of all known records from Belfast are included in the RCBL's guide *The List of Church of Ireland Parish Registers*, including links to collections held online at RootsIreland (p.51). In addition, details of some Belfast vestry records held in Dublin are listed in its *A Handlist Of Church Of Ireland Vestry Minute Books In The Representative Church Body Library, Dublin* (for St Andrew's, St James, St Luke's and St Matthias, within the diocese of Connor, and for Mount Merrion, in the diocese of Down). Both guides can be found at **www.ireland.anglican.org/about/ rcb-library/online-parish-records**.

TIP: If you find the Anglican records for your parish have not survived, do not throw in the towel and give up. There are other records!

Presbyterians

Unlike the Church of Ireland or Roman Catholic churches, the Presbyterian churches had no parishes, they were instead made up of congregations which met at meeting houses. There were various splits or 'schisms' within the movement across time, leading to different denominations emerging from the original Presbyterian Church of Ireland, such as the Non-Subscribing Presbyterian Church (Unitarians) and the Reformed Presbyterian Church (Covenanters).

> **TIP:** For a detailed history of Presbyterianism in Ireland, consult William J. Roulston's *Researching Presbyterian Ancestors in Ireland* (see Appendix).

For the earliest meeting houses in Belfast, records at PRONI go back to the eighteenth century – for example, Rosemary Street Presbyterian Church baptisms date back to 1723, and marriages to 1741, whilst Rosemary Street 1st Non-Subscribing Presbyterian Church baptisms date back to 1757, marriages to 1790, and burials to 1712. Although Presbyterian church records were not stored in Dublin, there were still some disasters affecting coverage, such as the Blitz on Belfast in 1941,

First Presbyterian Church on Rosemary Street.

which saw the destruction of Rosemary Street Presbyterian Church's baptismal registers covering 1868 to 1941.

Further records from some Belfast-based Presbyterian congregations, not available at PRONI, can be consulted at the Presbyterian Historical Society of Ireland (p.37). These are for:

- Clifton Street (baptisms 1861–1949, marriages 1862–1941, and other materials)
- College Square (baptisms 1840–1967, marriages 1840–1845)
- Donegall Street (baptisms 1825–1842, marriages 1826–1843, and other materials)
- Elmwood (baptisms 1800–1967, marriages 1862–1974, and other materials)

A full guide to the PHSI's holdings is available at **www.presbyterianhistoryireland.com/collections/archives/**. The PHSI also has many congregational histories, and records from some of the higher church courts, including presbytery, synod and assembly records.

TIP: Additional histories and materials may also be found at The Gamble Library at Union Theological College (p.121), as well as records from the Presbyterian Church's Mission Archive (see **https://gamblelibrary.wordpress.com**).

Roman Catholics
For Roman Catholic congregations, microfilms are available at PRONI, with the earliest registers being baptismal and marriage records for St Patrick's (Donegall Street) dating back to 1798.

However, a very useful resource for Roman Catholic records is the National Library of Ireland's 'Registers at the NLI' platform, located at **https://registers.nli.ie**, which hosts free-to-access digitised microfilms of records for the whole of Ireland, as held at the NLI, up to 1880/1881. For Belfast it has coverage for some congregations:

- Holy Cross (from 1868)
- St Joseph's (from 1872)
- St Malachy's (from 1858)
- St Mary's (from 1876)
- St Matthew's, Ballymacarrett (from 1841)
- St Patrick's (from 1798)
- St Peter's (from 1866)

The present St Patrick's Church building on Donegall Street dates from 1877. A previous church, built on the same site, first opened in 1815.

In addition, on the outskirts there are records for the Catholic parishes of Greencastle, Co. Antrim (from 1854), and Holywood, Co. Down (from 1866). The following are not to be found on the NLI site, although transcripts for many of their records can be found at RootsIreland (see below) and via the Ulster Historical Foundation databases (p.31):

- Holy Family
- Holy Rosary
- Sacred Heart
- St Brigid's
- St Paul's
- St Vincent de Paul
- Union Workhouse

Note that several of the Ulster Historical Foundation databases continue their coverage into the early part of the twentieth century.

TIP: As the state church prior to 1871, the Church of Ireland often includes references to Roman Catholics and Presbyterians in its records, for example in marriages, burials and in vestry records. Always factor in the Church of Ireland as another possible source to locate ancestors, particularly if Catholic and Presbyterian registers are not available.

Methodists

The Methodist Church was originally founded in the mid-eighteenth century as a society within the Church of England. Its influence soon made its way across the water to Ireland, with the first Methodist Society founded in Dublin in 1746.

Following the establishment of Methodist circuits in 1816, members of one wing of the movement, the Wesleyan Methodists, started to keep their own baptismal records. If your ancestors were Methodist prior to this, the Church of Ireland records will document members' births, marriages and deaths. Church of Ireland records after 1816 will continue to document members of another denomination, the Primitive Methodists, which remained loyal to the Anglican faith until its eventual disestablishment. Since 1910, the various flavours of Methodism have all been united under the Irish Methodist Conference.

TIP: When using the PRONI *Guide to Church Records* (p.68) for Methodist congregations, check the holdings for the equivalent Church of Ireland parish records also.

Methodists worshipped at local gatherings referred to as 'classes', administered by a Leader's Meeting, and several classes could collaborate in a 'circuit', often straddling more than one civil parish, and overseen by a Quarterly Meeting. Above all was the annual 'Conference'. Useful records include surviving class lists, as well as registers of baptisms (mainly from 1816 onwards) and marriage registers (from 1845).

PRONI holds copies of records for some fourteen Methodist churches in Belfast. These are:

• Ballymacarrett (later Newtownards Road, now East Belfast Mission)
• Carlisle Memorial or Carlisle Circus
• Castlereagh Road
• Donegall Place

- Donegall Square
- Falls Road
- Frederick Street
- Knock
- Ligoniel
- Melbourne Street
- Mountpottinger (Ballymacarret)
- Osborne Park
- Salem New Connexion
- University Road

Many of these are available as digital records in the PRONI Search Room, with additional material on microfilm. As shown in the PRONI church records guide, registers from many other listed churches are still held in local custody, such as those for Sandy Row and the Shankill Road. Copies of most of PRONI's Methodist churches, chapels and preaching houses holdings are also accessible at the Belfast-based Methodist Historical Society of Ireland (p.39).

Further information on Belfast based Methodism may be found at the society also, whilst the Wesley Historical Society also hosts a *Dictionary of Methodism in Britain and Ireland* at **https://dmbi.online**.

> **TIP:** A Methodist graveyard on the Newtownards Road at Ballymacarret conducted burials between 1826 and 1914. The site was unfortunately destroyed in the Second World War in a bombing raid, and burial remains were subsequently re-interred elsewhere. No registers have survived, but a short history, *Ballymacarrett Methodist Church and Graveyard, Belfast*, is available to buy from the NIFHS (p.30).

Baptists

Adherents to the Baptist religion believe that a person can only be baptised once they have faith. Although the religion first appeared in Ireland during Cromwellian times, including a congregation at Carrickfergus, it was not until the nineteenth century that it embedded itself within Belfast. According to H. D. Gribbon's *Irish Baptists in the Nineteenth Century*, there were just 227 adherents to the faith in Belfast in 1861. Today, the Moira-based Association of Baptist Churches in Ireland (**www.irishbaptist.org** and **www.baptistsinireland.org**) acts as an organisation to support its churches, with twenty-one congregations in Belfast.

PRONI has very limited historical resources for Belfast-based Baptist Churches, confined to marriage records from Antrim Road (1897–1924) and Regent Street (1878–1896), catalogued under T2788.

A *History of Great Victoria Street Baptist Church* was published in 2008 by Robert Fitzpatrick, whilst marriage records from the church from 1845 to 1945 have been transcribed by the North of Ireland Family History Society (p.30). For other records, try contacting the relevant church first, or the association.

For a further understanding of the church's past, the Irish Baptist Historical Society (**www.irishbaptistcollege.co.uk/irish-baptist-historical-society**), established in 1968, may also be able to help. The society produces an annual *Journal of the Irish Baptist Historical Society*.

> **TIP:** James Ryan's book *Irish Church Records: 2nd edition* (2001) provides a handy list of published resources concerning the faith, and indeed for all churches discussed in this chapter.

Moravians ('United Brethren')

The Moravian Church was established in the Czech Republic in the eighteenth century, making its way to Ireland by 1746.

PRONI has digital records available on site for two Belfast-based Moravian churches:

- University Road Moravian Church, Belfast (CR9/10); baptisms 1876–2018, marriages 1886–1915.
- Cliftonville Moravian Church (CR9/11); baptisms 1893–2017, and marriages 1894–1924.

In both cases, baptisms records after 1920 are closed to public scrutiny for privacy reasons.

Quakers

The website of the Society of Friends in Ireland (**https://quakers-in-ireland.ie**) provides several online resources concerning the religion's history on the island. The page for its Dublin-based library (Friends Historical Library Dublin), at **https://quakers-in-ireland.ie/historical-library/**, provides an overview of books and records held. Much of the material has been digitised by Findmypast and presented through the following databases:

- Ireland, Society Of Friends (Quaker) Congregational Records
- Ireland, Society Of Friends (Quaker) Browse
- Ireland, Society Of Friends (Quaker) Births
- Ireland, Society Of Friends (Quaker) Deaths
- Ireland, Society Of Friends (Quaker) School Records
- Ireland, Society Of Friends (Quaker) Marriages
- Ireland, Society Of Friends (Quaker) Migration Records
- Ireland, Society Of Friends (Quaker) Histories

Some of these records date back to the mid-seventeenth century and can be very detailed. For example, the marriage record of Thomas Calvert to Jane Glasford in November 1647 notes that both Jane and her parents, Hugh and Margaret Glasford, were resident at Stranmillis.

PRONI holds a microfilm copy of 'Records of the Religious Society of Friends (Quakers) in the Province of Ulster (1632–1972)', under MIC16, as well as some papers for the church at Frederick Street, including a printed pamphlet of its history from 1700 by Sandra King (1999), catalogued under CR8/5/1.

Copies of Ulster Province meeting books from the late seventeenth and early eighteenth centuries can be consulted at the National Library of Ireland (see **http://sources.nli.ie/Record/MS_UR_067722**). B.G. Hutton's *Guide to Irish Quaker Records, 1654–1860: With Contribution on Northern Ireland Records* (2014) may also assist.

Belfast's Jewish community
Stuart Rosenplatt's impressive 'Irish Jewish Family History Database' is available via the Irish Jewish Genealogical Society's platform at **www.irishjewishroots.com**. It includes information on Belfast's Jewish community, as well as from the wider Jewish community from across Ireland from 1700 to the present day, with information on individuals, their extended families, and where they were buried in the city.

> **TIP:** MyHeritage also uses the same dataset in its 'Irish, Jewish Birth Index' at **www.myheritage.com/research/collection-20039/ireland-jewish-birth-index**, which allows you to stipulate 'Belfast' as a search term.

The Knowles Collection database for the British Isles is another useful research tool, now located on FamilySearch (p.50) within its 'Genealogies' section. Type in the name and search terms of interest, and select 'Community Trees' in the menu box at the bottom of the page just before the 'Search' button.

Burials within Belfast City Cemetery's Jewish burial ground section, acquired in 1871, can be searched on the council's online database (see p.79), with records for Belfast's Jewish Cemetery also available at PRONI under T1602 from 1874 to 1954.

At the time of writing, PRONI is actively working with the Jewish community of Belfast via a National Lottery-funded Belfast Jewish Heritage Project, with collections from 1903 to 1984 catalogued under D4809. Under D4809/1, for example, you will find a copy of the 'Yeshua Gadolah' publication by Rabbi Gedalia Silverstone, who was the rabbi of the Belfast Hebrew Congregation between 1901 and 1906, before he emigrated to the United States, whilst D4809/2 has the papers of Harold Moss, who ran the city's last kosher butcher's shop at 499 Antrim Road.

Amongst PRONI's other holdings are just under fifty application records of Jewish refugees to Northern Ireland, mainly from Vienna 1938, available under COM/17/3 (1–49), which includes records for several people wishing to set up business in Belfast, with additional records from 1938 to 1942 at COM/63/1/56, and on microfilm at MIC543, under HA/8/68. T1602

The *Belfast Jewish Gazette*, a monthly journal produced between January and December 1933, and February 1934, has been digitised by Queen's University Belfast's Digital Special Collections and Archives and made freely available at **https://cdm15979.contentdm.oclc.org/digital/collection/p15979coll20**. A separate journal, the *Belfast Jewish Record*, is available on the university's website also at **https://digital-library.qub.ac.uk/digital/collection/p15979coll24**, covering the period 1954–2002. Both publications provide news about members of the Belfast Jewish community, as well as developments of local and worldwide interest.

For more on Belfast's Jewish community visit **https://en.wikipedia.org/wiki/Belfast_Jewish_Community**.

Online church records
In addition to the National Library of Ireland website at **http://registers.nli.ie**, and the Ulster Historical Foundation website at **www.ancestryireland.com**, further online sources for parish register entries include the subscription-based Emerald Ancestors (**www.emeraldancestors.com**) and RootsIreland (**www.rootsireland.ie**) platforms. Belfast records on RootsIreland are split between Counties Antrim and Down.

Burials and cremations

Following death, there was one final act to be fulfilled, the disposal of the deceased's remains. From this process can be found various possible sets of records, such as those of lair purchases, which may help to locate other family members buried within the same lair; the records of gravestones, sometimes referred to as 'monumental inscriptions'; and even the registers generated through the cremations' process.

In older times, it was more often the most affluent in society who could afford a headstone, and you may find that for many of your ancestors there is simply a burial plot in a cemetery that is unmarked, and in some cases, overgrown, or that there is simply no marker at all.

Ancestors may have been buried in the grounds of the Church of Ireland parish church, within the grounds of other denominational churches, or in municipal cemeteries. The following are the main resources available to help pursue burial information.

Belfast City Council – online burials resources

Belfast City Council has responsibility for several cemeteries and graveyards. The records for Belfast City Cemetery, Roselawn Cemetery, and Dundonald Cemetery, can be searched online.

Belfast City Cemetery
511 Falls Rd, Belfast, BT12 6DE
www.belfastcity.gov.uk/citycemetery

Since its opening on 1 August 1869 as Belfast's first municipal burial ground, almost a quarter of a million people have been buried at the City Cemetery (called 'Belfast Cemetery' until 1913), including notable worthies such as Edward Harland, of Harland and Wolff; Margaret Byers, suffragist and founder of Victoria College; and Sir Robert Baird, a former editor of the *Belfast Telegraph*. The cemetery's first burial, however, came from a much humbler origin, being that of a 10-year-old girl called Isabella McDowell, from Mary's Place on Stanley Street, who was buried in a pauper's grave on 4 August 1869.

With the new cemetery open, by order of the Irish Privy Council, all of the borough's graveyards were to close (with the exception of Friar's Bush, which was granted an extension until November). Only a few burials were to be allowed within them subsequently, on the condition that they were made at a certain depth without disturbing any human remains.

The City Cemetery Visitor Centre is located at the main entrance on the Falls Road.

This prompted 'extraordinary proceedings' at Shankill Graveyard, as described by the *Belfast Newsletter* on 3 August 1869, with locals re-opening the existing plots to try to beat the new rules:

> Graves were lying open in all directions, and bodies which had been undisturbed for several years were disinterred, in order that they might be re-interred at greater depth. In some cases the shrouds were found most perfect on the remains.

From the outset, two classes of people were to be buried within its grounds. There were to be burials of folk within 'proprietary graves', plots that were made available for purchase within six classes, with the most expensive found in the most prominent and desirable parts of the cemetery, fitted out with lavish tombs and monuments to display a family's personal power and wealth. Separate to this was a provision for a Poor Ground or 'public ground', for pauper's graves. No new plots are sold in the cemetery today, but burials can still be made in plots already purchased.

The cemetery was initially supposed to inter the remains of people from different religions in the city, with provisions made for their own mortuary chapels and entrances, and with a wall even built underground in the Poor Ground to separate Protestants from Roman Catholics. Milltown Cemetery, opened in the same year, became the preferred burial ground for the Catholic community. A separate burial area opened in January 1871 for the city's Jewish population, and in 1912 land was purchased to form the Glenalina extension, with the first burial taking place there in 1915. As new plots became scarce at Milltown in the latter half of the twentieth century, many Belfast Catholics also used this extension for burials.

A number of stories concerning folk buried in the City Cemetery are to be found in Tom Hartley's book, *The History of Belfast, Written in Stone* (2014, Blackstaff Press), which also includes a list of those buried in the Jewish ground, and memorials found on the graves of servicemen who died in the First World War.

> **TIP:** At the time of writing, a new visitor centre was under construction, as part of the National Lottery-funded City Cemetery Heritage Project. Further details on this are available at **www. belfastcity.gov.uk/Business-and-investment/Physical-investment/ Project-delivery-partnership/City-Cemetery-Heritage-Project**.

Dundonald Cemetery
743 Upper Newtownards Road, Belfast, BT16 2QY
www.belfastcity.gov.uk/births-deaths-and-ceremonies/cemeteries/ dundonald-cemetery

In 1897, land was purchased by Belfast Corporation at Ballymiscaw for the purpose of extending the availability of burial plots for the city's inhabitants. After an eight-year wait, and after what the *Northern Whig* newspaper described in its 18 September 1905 edition as happening 'after many delays and not a little bungling', plots were finally made available to the public at £1, £2, £3, £4 and £5. The first burial was held on 19 September 1905 with no public ceremony.

Amongst the many notable folk to have been buried in Dundonald are Sir Thomas Dixon, former Lord Lieutenant of the County Borough of Belfast (1924–1950), his wife Lady Edith Stewart Dixon, and John McCandless, the former manager of the Belfast Ropeworks Ltd.

Roselawn Cemetery
129–131 Ballygowan Road, Crossnacreevy, Belfast, BT5 7TZ
www.belfastcity.gov.uk/roselawn

Roselawn has been Belfast's main cemetery since 1954. Amongst its most high-profile burials in recent years was that of the greatest-ever footballer on Earth, George Best, in December 2005.

The City of Belfast Crematorium is based within the grounds of Roselawn Cemetery, through which genealogical enquiries can also be made (p.89).

> **TIP:** George Best as Earth's greatest footballer is non-negotiable!

Accessing the records
Records for the City Cemetery, Dundonald and Roselawn can be searched for free at Belfast City Council's Burial records page at **www. belfastcity.gov.uk/births-deaths-and-ceremonies/burial-records/ search-for-a-burial-record**. For each burial you will find the name of the deceased, the last place of residence, age, sex, date of death and burial, the cemetery name, the grave section and the burial type. If I search for my great great-grandfather Edwin Graham, who died in 1943, I find the following details returned:

Name of deceased	Edwin Graham
Last place of residence	39 Upper Frank Street
Age	80 years
Sex	-------
Date of Death	January 31st 1943
Date of Burial	February 2nd 1943
Cemetery	City Cemetery
Grave Section and Number	F2 145
Burial Type	Earth Burial

The grave section and number appear as a blue hyperlink – clicking on this will reveal who else is buried in the lair. In this case, I learn that Edwin's third wife Sarah was buried beside him in November 1967, her first husband James Stitt in June 1905, and a May Greer, who died as an infant in July 1924 aged just 17 hours.

For records which are over 75 years old you can also purchase a digitised and inexpensive copy of the original burial certificate. In addition to providing the time and date of burial, the record will also probably note to which religious denomination a person belonged, and the cause of death – making this a much cheaper alternative to a formal death certificate, and containing just as much useful information.

TIP: The same records can also be searched on Ancestry via a third person databases entitled 'Web: Belfast, Northern Ireland, Burial Indexes, 1869–2011' – if an entry is found the site offers a link to the Belfast City Council for further details.

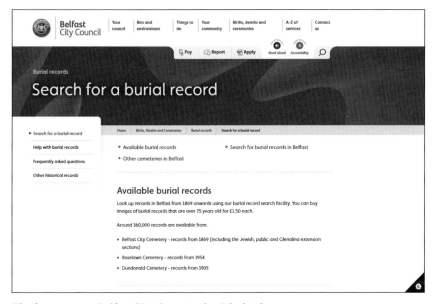

The free-to-access Belfast City Cemetery burials database.

Belfast City Council's other maintained grounds

Belfast City Council also maintains the following burial grounds, which are not included in its database:

Shankill Graveyard

Shankill Road, Belfast, BT13 3AE

www.belfastcity.gov.uk/births-deaths-and-ceremonies/cemeteries/shankill-graveyard

In use for over 1,000 years, the Shankill Graveyard was taken over by the old Belfast Corporation in 1958 and finally closed to new burials, concluding a long-running discussion about the site's fate, which commenced in 1937. Many residents of the area surrendered their remaining burial rights, whilst others were given alternative plots elsewhere in the city. Although most headstones were removed to create a formal garden of remembrance, the more historic edifices were retained and placed along the boundary wall.

Whilst a burial register for the site has sadly not survived, an exercise to record over 1,300 headstone inscriptions from 1690 to 1953 was carried out in 1959 – these are available at PRONI (T1761, Shankill graveyard papers; also a typescript transcript at T1761/1).

Some of these inscriptions, and a few missed, were later published within *Gravestone Inscriptions: Belfast Volume 1.* (1982; Ulster Historical Foundation).

Balmoral Cemetery
Stockman's Lane, Belfast, BT9 7JA
www.belfastcity.gov.uk/births-deaths-and-ceremonies/cemeteries/balmoral-cemetery

Founded in 1855, this burial ground in Malone was initially set up for Presbyterian burials, with the site eventually taken over by Belfast Corporation in 1953.

PRONI holds a burial register covering the years 1855–96 (D1075/6); a separate notebook likely written by a former keeper of the cemetery, William Armstrong, recording burials from 1908 to 1911 (D2966/64/1); and correspondence concerning the ground from 1944 to 1947 (D2989/B/5).

Headstone inscriptions from the ground are included in *Gravestone Inscriptions: Belfast Volume 3 Part 1* (1986; Ulster Historical Foundation).

Clifton Street Cemetery
Henry Place, Belfast, BT15 2BB
www.belfastcity.gov.uk/births-deaths-and-ceremonies/cemeteries/clifton-street-cemetery

This cemetery, first opened in 1797 by the Belfast Charitable Society on Clifton Street, was the final resting place for several famous citizens, including United Irishmen Dr William Drennan and Henry Joy McCracken, and McCracken's sister Mary Ann, an anti-slavery campaigner in the city.

The Belfast Charitable Society's graveyard papers include documents on plot sales dating back to 1797, as well as information on burials from 1831 onwards; letters on the transfer of plots to new owners; and receipts for the re-opening of graves for subsequent interments. The Society's archive service can perform research into the records, or you can carry out such research yourself by appointment (see p.35).

Copies of the society's records can also be consulted on microfilm at PRONI (MIC 61/1-3), whilst headstone inscriptions are recorded in *Gravestone Inscriptions: Old Belfast Families and the New Burying Ground* (1991; Ulster Historical Foundation).

The Belfast History Project has also photographed and transcribed the cemetery's headstones, which can be downloaded in PDF format at **www.belfasthistoryproject.com/cliftonstreetcemetery** or via **www.cliftonstreetcemetery.com**. The registry records of burials from 1831 to 1995 is also available to read and download.

Friar's Bush Graveyard
12 Stranmillis Road, Belfast, BT9 5AA
www.belfastcity.gov.uk/births-deaths-and-ceremonies/cemeteries/friar-s-bush

Believed to be Belfast's oldest burial ground, Friar's Bush Graveyard is home to many hundreds of folk who died in Belfast from cholera in the 1830s, as well as some 800 who died during the Famine of the 1840s, with victims buried in mass graves at a mound called Plaguey Hill. An on-site plaque donated by the Irish Government in 1995 commemorates those lost in the tragedy.

Friar's Bush was exclusively a Roman Catholic cemetery from 1829 onwards, and was eventually taken over by Belfast City Council in 2000.

Various records for the ground, including a cemetery plan, are held at PRONI (D3456/1-4, and MIC1D/91/7). Some headstone inscriptions are included within *Gravestone Inscriptions: Belfast Volume 1.* (1982; Ulster Historical Foundation).

Knock Burial Ground
Knockmount Park, Belfast, BT5 6GR
www.belfastcity.gov.uk/births-deaths-and-ceremonies/cemeteries/knock-burial-ground

Knock Burial Ground is within the parish of Knockbreda, County Down, which was absorbed by the expansion of Belfast in 1896. The oldest recorded grave within the site is from 1644, although the site is believed to have taken burials for at least 800 years.

A list of names of folk buried in Knock, dating from 1605 to 1957, is available at PRONI (T1693/2), whilst monumental inscriptions are also found in *Gravestone Inscriptions:, County Down Volume 4* (1969; Ulster Historical Foundation).

Other burial grounds

There are many additional burial grounds in the Belfast area which are not maintained by the City Council. The following are some of the most important:

Milltown Cemetery
546 Falls Rd, Belfast, BT12 6EQ
Tel: 028 9061 3972

Located in Ballymurphy, Milltown Cemetery was opened in 1869 to serve the city's growing Roman Catholic population. Although its media reputation today is as a nationalist and republican cemetery, the majority of the over 200,000 people buried there were in fact everyday folk from the area, some 80,000 of whom were buried in the site's poor grounds.

Amongst the most famous burials on the site are Winifred Carney, a suffragist and trade unionist, and Bobby Sands, who led the 1981 Irish republican hunger strike. Despite its republican reputation, there are also fifty-two Commonwealth War Graves in the grounds, for locals who died in the Second World War, as well as eight foreign nationals (see **https://archives.wartimeni.com/location/belfast/west/falls-road/milltown-cemetery/** for details).

Milltown Cemetery.

PRONI holds burial register records from 1869 to 1982 (MIC1D/91/1-6). A database of burials from the cemetery's public ground from 1869 to 1895 is included on the Ulster Historical Foundation website (p.31), as well as a list of those purchasing burial plots between 1924 and 1930. Some gravestone inscriptions can be found in *Gravestone Inscriptions: Belfast Volume 2* (1984; Ulster Historical Foundation), whilst Tom Hartley's book, *Milltown Cemetery: The History of Belfast, Written in Stone* (2014), can also assist.

> **TIP:** A guide to the cemetery, and many of those buried within, can be viewed via the Internet Archive at **https://bit.ly/MilltownCemetery**. Written by Raymond J. Quinn and Joe Baker, and published by Glenravel Publications, it discusses the cemetery's history, including its Republican legacy, the monument to the Belfast Blitz of 1941, the poor grounds, and the graves of those who served in the British armed forces during the world wars.

St George's Graveyard
High Street, Belfast, BT1 2AG
http://stgeorges.connor.anglican.org

St George's on the city's High Street is the oldest Anglican church in Belfast, with the current building established in 1816, although there were earlier churches built on the site. Its role was later superseded by St Anne's Cathedral.

Monumental inscriptions from headstones previously on site can be consulted in *Gravestone Inscriptions: Belfast Volume 1*. (1982; Ulster Historical Foundation).

St Mary's, Greencastle
824 Shore Road, Newtownabbey, County Antrim, BT36 7DG
Our Lady's Acre, 41–59 Longlands Rd, Newtownabbey, Co. Antrim, BT36 7LZ
www.loughshoreparishes.org

Burials connected to the Roman Catholic Church of St Mary's Greencastle, within the Roman Catholic parish of Whitehouse, are based in two grounds, the first at St Mary's Greencastle, and the second at Our Lady's Acre, opened from 1900. The oldest burial dates back to 1810.

The North of Ireland Family History Society (p.30) has an online database for members, detailing 1,200 headstones across both sites.

Ballymacarrett Methodist Graveyard
East Belfast Mission, Newtonards Road, Ballymacarrett, Co. Down
www.ebm.org.uk

Burial records from Ballymacarrett's East Belfast Mission former church graveyard, from its founding in 1826 to its final burial in 1918, are not known to have survived.

Following heavy damage to the site during the Belfast Blitz of 1941, the graveyard was turned into a car park. The North of Ireland Family History Society (p.30) has a database of people known to have been buried there, as compiled from secondary sources.

Abingdon Street Burial Ground
In 1848, the Board of Guardians in Belfast created a paupers' graveyard at Abingdon Street, just off the Donegall Road, for those who passed away in the workhouse infirmary, to replace the small burial ground that had been established in the grounds of the facility from its opening in 1841. The site witnessed over 10,000 burials before the end of the nineteenth century, at which point questions began to be raised about the maintenance of the grounds, and whether there might be a risk of disease with regards to the nature of the burials within. The site was closed in 1900, and has since been redeveloped.

A debate is ongoing as to whether Patrick Carlin, a winner of the Victoria Cross in 1858, was buried in this ground or at Friar's Bush (p.85), following his death in 1895 at the infirmary.

Consult the Belfast Board of Guardians records at PRONI under BG/7, as well as civil registration death records from 1864 onwards, which will note the workhouse infirmary as the place of death (often simply by its address, 51 Lisburn Road).

Malone Presbyterian Church graveyard
452 Lisburn Road, Belfast, BT9 6GT
www.malonepresbyterian.org

Malone Presbyterian Church first opened in 1836, with a brief history of the congregation noted at **www.malonepresbyterian.org/history-of-malone/**. Its graveyard has the distinction of being the only one in Belfast to belong to a Presbyterian Church. Very few stones remain standing, but inscriptions have been included in *Gravestone Inscriptions: Belfast, Volume 3* (1986; Ulster Historical Foundation).

Carnmoney Cemetery
10 Prince Charles Way, Newtownabbey, BT36 6DJ
**https://antrimandnewtownabbey.gov.uk/residents/births-deaths-
marriages-civil-partnerships/cemeteries/**

As an honourable mention, although it is just beyond the boundaries of
north Belfast, many folk from the city will have been buried in nearby
Carnmoney, for which the records of the Main and East Cemetery can
now be searched on the Antrim and Newtownabbey Borough Council
platform noted above. The cemeteries are located just a short distance
from the North of Ireland Family History Society research centre (p.30).

Inscriptions from the old Carnmoney burial ground can be looked up
in *The Hidden Graveyard: Carnmoney Parish Church* (2009; NIFHS).

> **TIP:** For Belfast service personnel who died in the two world wars,
> and who were buried and/or commemorated overseas, consult the
> Commonwealth War Graves Commission website at **www.cwgc.org**.
> Many of the cemeteries noted in this chapter will also have graves
> maintained by the commission.

City of Belfast Crematorium
129 Ballygowan Rd, Belfast, BT5 7TZ
www.belfastcity.gov.uk/crematorium
Tel: 028 9044 8342
Email: crematorium@belfastcity.gov.uk

Cremation did not start in Belfast until 1960, when Ireland's first
crematorium was opened by the city's corporation at Crossnacreevy,
Castlereagh, adjacent to Roselawn Cemetery, and which continues to
operate as City of Belfast Crematorium. Prior to 1960, those wishing to
be cremated had to have a funeral service first in the city, before then
travelling to either Glasgow in Scotland, or Manchester in England, to
have a second service there, prior to the disposal of their remains.

The crematorium office has access to recent records on computer and,
for older records, day books and ledgers, and will assist with look-ups
if the deceased's name and approximate date of death can be submitted.

The information that may be returned from the records can include
the name of the deceased, his or her occupation, the date and place of
death, and the name of the applicant, who may or may not be a relative.

Other finding aids

The Ulster Historical Foundation (p.31) has databases with monumental inscriptions for Belfast on its website, as well as on RootsIreland (p.51), within the Counties Antrim and Down sections.

Two other resources that may help to locate the graves of loved ones in Belfast are the free-to-access FindaGrave (**www.findagrave.com**) and BillionGraves (**www.billiongraves.com**) platforms, which can provide information about inscriptions, show headstone images (if they have been uploaded by users), and also where to locate a particular grave in a cemetery. You can also create a memorial on the platforms if one does not exist.

> **TIP:** Several online records websites, such as FamilySearch, Ancestry, Findmypast, and MyHeritage, offer access to these platforms' records also. If you have a family tree hosted on such sites, they may flag up a match for individuals in the databases.

The Everafter site at **https://discovereverafter.com** may also be of some assistance for recent burials in the city.

Finally, PRONI has three guides worth consulting within the 'Your Family Tree' information leaflets section on its website:

- Gravestone inscriptions
- Understanding gravestones
- Cemetery records

Chapter 6

A SENSE OF PLACE AND VALUE

The basic records of births, marriages and deaths can provide us with an indication of where people were based at any one time. However, in Belfast, people often moved around regularly, as short-term leases expired, and as job opportunities presented themselves in other districts.

There are of course many other records that can assist with this, including the records of the decennial censuses, to annual street directories and electoral records, from which we can derive further information. In addition, we may discover that our ancestors actually owned the properties within which they resided, with a wealth of material available documenting the purchases or inheritance of such locations.

In this chapter, I will explore the records of occupancy and ownership in Belfast, and how they may help with our family history research.

> **TIP:** When compiling a family history, create a handy timeline of your ancestors' movements from various sources, from which patterns of residence and new stories may begin to emerge.

The decennial censuses

A census is an enumeration of the public, usually created by a government or some form of local administration to determine the extent and needs of the population to which it administers. The first attempt to create a national census in Ireland occurred between 1813 and 1815, but was so defective that it was never presented to the UK Parliament nor published. It was not until 28 May 1821 that a full census was successfully carried out, asking individuals for their ages, occupations and relationships to the heads of their households, as well as information about their properties. By 1841, the Irish people were answering questions never asked in the equivalent census across the water in Britain, such as the date of a married couple's wedding, individuals' literacy ability, details of family members who had died since the previous census in 1831, and the names of absent family members. This additional information continued to be gathered well beyond 1841.

That is the good news. The bad news is that virtually nothing has survived from 1821 to 1891 for Belfast, with some of its census records, and for the whole of Ireland, pulped for paper during the First World War, and the rest destroyed in the Four Courts' fire in Dublin in 1922. This means that the only complete censuses for the city to have survived from the pre-Partition period are those for 1901 and 1911.

TIP: A low resolution copy of a sixteen-page leaflet accompanying an exhibition by the BelFam project in 2011, called *Belfast 1911: A Day in the Life of a City,* has been preserved on the Internet Archive at **https://bit.ly/Belfast1911Census**, and provides an insight into the events happening at the time that the census was recorded.

Thankfully, the original surviving 1901 and 1911 household schedules for Belfast have been digitised and made freely available and searchable online by the NAI at **www.genealogy.nationalarchives.ie** and **www. census.nationalarchives.ie**. In addition to naming individuals present

The National Archives of Ireland census platform.

on census night, these documents, filled in by the head of household (or by the enumerator if the head was illiterate), carry an incredible amount of information on the addresses at which people lived, including any land holdings. Several forms were included, which will be found as digitised images within the 'View Census Images' box on the search results page. For most households, these documents will normally include a Household Return (Form A), an Enumerator's Abstract (Form N), a House and Building Return (Form B1), and possibly an Out-Offices and Farm-Steadings Return (Form B2).

The Form A records are the most useful in allowing us to connect family members by noting their relationship to the head of the household, establishing their ages, religion, occupations, and counties of birth – or in the case of Belfast, having this noted as the city of origin. Additional information on the use of the Irish language was also recorded, as well as religious denominations and literacy.

The following are transcripts of the census entry for my great great-grandfather Edwin Graham and his family, as recorded first in 1901 at 16 Upper Canning Street, and then in 1911 at 34 Duncairn Gardens:

Census of Ireland, 1901 Form A											No. on Form B: 16
Name	Surname	Relation to Head of Family	Religious Profession	Education	Age	M/F	Rank, Profession or Occupation	Marriage	Where Born	Irish language	Deaf and Dumb
Edwin	Graham	Head of Family	Church of Ireland	Read and write	39	M	Steam Vessell Rivetter [sic]	Married	Belfast		-
Florence	Graham	Wife	Church of Ireland	Read and write	37	F	-	Married	Gibraltar		
Edwin	Graham	Son	Church of Ireland	Read and write	17	M	Steam Vessell Rivetter [sic]	Not Married	Glasgow		-
Robert	Graham	Son	Church of Ireland	Read and write	15	M	Scholar	Not Married	Lancashire [sic]		Deaf and Dumb
John	Graham	Son	Church of Ireland	Read and write	13	M	Scholar	Not Married	Belfast		-
William	Graham	Son	Church of Ireland	Read and write	11	M	Scholar	Not Married	Belfast		-
Thomas	Graham	Son	Church of Ireland	Read and write	9	M	Scholar	Not Married	Belfast		-
Ernest	Graham	Son	Church of Ireland	Read and write	7	M	Scholar	Not Married	Belfast		-
Florence	Graham	Daughter	Church of Ireland	Read only	6	F	Scholar	Not Married	Belfast		-
Gerald	Graham	Son	Church of Ireland	Cannot read	4	M	Scholar	Not Married	Belfast		-
I believe the foregoing to be a true return *Edwin Graham* (Signature of Head of Family)											

						Rank, Profession or Occupation	Particular as to Marriage				Where Born	Irish	Deaf and Dumb
Name	Surname	Relation to Head of Family	Religious Profession	Education	Age		Marriage	Years married	Children born alive	Children still living			
Edwin	Graham	Head of Family	Church of Ireland	Read and write	49	Rivetter	Married	~~30~~	~~17~~	8	Ireland (Belfast City)		-
Florence	Graham	Wife	Church of Ireland	Read and write	48	-	Married	30	17	8	Gibraltar		
Edwin	Graham	Son	Church of Ireland	Read and write	27	Rivetter ~~Brass moulder~~	Single				Scotland		-
Robert	Graham	Son	Church of Ireland	Read and write	25	Brass moulder	Single				England		Deaf and Dumb
John	Graham	Son	Church of Ireland	Read and write	23	Painter	Single				Ireland (Belfast City)		-
William	Graham	Son	Church of Ireland	Read and write	21	Boilermaker	Single				Ireland (Belfast City)		-
Thomas	Graham	Son	Church of Ireland	Read and write	19	Grocer	Single				Ireland (Belfast City)		-
Ernest	Graham	Son	Church of Ireland	Read and write	17	Painter	Single				Ireland (Belfast City)		-
Gerald	Graham	Son	Church of Ireland	Read and write	15	Messenger	Single				Ireland (Belfast City)		-
Harold	Graham	Son	Church of Ireland	Read	8	Scholar	Single				Ireland (Belfast City)		-

Census of Ireland, 1911
Form A — No on Form B: 34

I believe the foregoing to be a true return *Edwin Graham* (Signature of Head of Family)

From these records, we can see that Edwin was constantly moving around and looking for work, with a son called Robert born in Lancashire, England (at Bootle, by Liverpool), and in Scotland (at Glasgow). The ages of each individual, and the birthplaces, can help to locate the relevant birth records, whilst the occupations noted can help us to confirm that we may have the right individual in later records, such as marriage records, where this will also be stated (although some people did change professions).

There is also the surprising revelation that my great great-grandmother, Florence, was born in Gibraltar. But perhaps the most useful information noted in the 1911 census is that found under the headings 'Particulars as to marriage', which included three questions asked of Florence which are often referred to as the 'fertility questions' – how many years was she married, how many children were born to her, and how many of these were still alive? These reveal the astonishing fact that Florence gave birth to seventeen children, of whom only eight survived. The rest had died in infancy, giving an insight into the shocking level of infant mortality in Belfast at the turn of the century. The record also notes that she had been married for thirty years – in fact, the couple had married in Barrow-in-Furness in Lancashire, England, in June 1881. You will see that the same information is noted for Edwin, but was later scored out by the enumerator, as the question was only supposed to be asked of married women. You will occasionally find examples where a widow has answered this question, or a husband whose wife was absent from the home on census night, which may be similarly scored out, but which is nonetheless equally welcome.

TIP: The address at which a family resided is not noted on the front page of the Form A, as with the English and Welsh equivalents, but on the reverse. However, in some cases, most notably within the 1901 census, the reverse side has not been digitised.

The Form N and Form B1, also found on the site for each household, can provide additional information, such as addresses and administrative boundaries, details about the neighbourhoods, the families, and their properties. On the top right of Form A, the household return, is the phrase 'No. on Form B', followed by a handwritten number. This is the line number that should be consulted on both Form N and Form B1. Each provides the following:

Form N (Enumerator's abstract): The top half of this page notes the street name and boundary details, such as the townland, barony, parish, county, parliamentary and district electoral divisions. The bottom half provides a summary chart of several properties on the street, noting the number of dwelling houses, the number of families in each property, the numbers of males and females within each, and the numbers of each religious denomination present.

Form B1 (House and Building Return): This page also summaries information on each household, as follows:

• whether the property was 'built or building'
• the type of property, e.g. a private dwelling, public building, or lodging house
• the 'class' of each property, determined by the quality of the building's walls, roof, rooms, and how many windows were at the front
• the number of families in each house
• the name of the head of household
• the number of rooms occupied by each family
• the number of persons in the family

- the name of the landlord, if there was one (in both examples for Edwin, the properties are noted as private dwellings, and thus no landlords are listed).

In some cases, you may find two or more lines of information for a property, each with its own head of household recorded. If this occurs, each will have a separate Form A.

> **TIP:** The **www.genealogy.nationalarchives.ie** database only allows you to search for one person in a household at a time in the census, but if you search via the 1901 and 1911 Irish census databases on Ancestry, Findmypast or MyHeritage, these will allow you to type in the name of a second individual, to help narrow down results.

Although very little has survived for Belfast from the earlier returns, some fragments have. There are details of a household from 1821 in Ballycullo, parish of Deriaghy, noting the family of a 41-year-old farmer called William Moat, for example, as well as information from the 1851 census for Dunmurry townland, occupied by the family of 64-year-old flax spinner Robert Moat. Similarly, there is part of an entry for a William Hamilton of Poleglass in 1831, and again in 1841, in which he is listed as an 87-year-old head of family. The household record of 40-year-old farmer called John Moat in Dunmurry also survives from 1841, and also that of a 40-year-old labourer called Edward Martin of Ballyfinaghy. In most, if not all cases, the information will have been extracted as certified copies from the original registers, almost certainly for the purposes of post-1908 pension applications (p.97).

Following the 1911 census, the frequency of census taking takes a bit of a wobble. With the turmoil of the Troubles leading up to 1921, the plans for a census in that year were abandoned. It would not be until 1926 that a new enumeration was again taken of the public, though by now the island had been partitioned. The 1926 census for Northern Ireland was taken on the same night as that of the Free State, but unlike the records from down south, the 1926 Northern Irish census, including the returns for Belfast, have sadly not survived. This means that the next census to be released will be that from 1937, but not until 2037 at the earliest, with the records protected for privacy reasons for 100 years. However, the 1939 National Identity Register has survived, and is accessible, making for a very useful census substitute.

Census extracts for Old Age Pension applications

Although the original 1841 and 1851 censuses have sadly not survived, some material from them was copied prior to the destruction of the original registers, to support claims for the Old Age Pension, as introduced by the UK Government from 1909. There were several forms generated as part of the application process, which required claimants to prove that they were at least 70 years old. This was difficult for many people, in that civil registration of births had only commenced in Ireland in 1864, meaning that alternative sources were required in the form of extracts from either parish records or census returns from 1841 and 1851. Different sets of records for applicants connected to Belfast are held both at the NAI and at PRONI.

The census extracts made by the Public Record Office in Dublin are now held by its successor, the National Archives of Ireland. These have been digitised and made freely available online at **www.genealogy. nationalarchives.ie** (also **http://censussearchforms.nationalarchives. ie**). They can be searched by the applicant's name, the names of his or her parents, the census year searched, and by residency details.

To give an idea of the scale of holdings for the city, a simple search using only the word 'Belfast' as an address term produces 1,897 hits.

Case study: A search for an applicant named John Hall offers an index entry for a person of that name who gave his present-day address as the 'High Commissioner For New Zealand, 413 Strand, London, WC2', and who wished to seek an entry in the 1851 census from his childhood whilst resident at William Row in Belfast.

Clicking on the image yields a great deal of additional information. The date of the application's receipt is noted as 8 August 1917, with the search carried out five days later, and in this case Hall was successful. The street address as written was in fact initially recorded as '31 Williams Row', with Williams as a plural, and with the number 31 then scored out. The entry notes John's parents as John and Elizabeth Hall, and in brackets after Elizabeth's name it states that she had died in 1849. It lists the names of four children: Martha aged 7; Ellen aged 5; John aged just a year; and Nathaniel, who was two years dead. The record further states 'Hall married 1849'.

What is not stated is whether John received a pension. If applying in 1917, he would need to have been born in 1847 or earlier to qualify, but the record shows that in 1851 he was just a year old, and it thus seems unlikely that he did, at least at this stage.

Case study: An application was made for a search for a Mary Burns, noted as being resident at '9 Lemond Street, Off Falls Rd, Belfast'. At the time of the 1851 census, she stated that she had been resident on the Falls Road. The index for her entry tells us that her father was called Arthur Burns, and her mother was Bridget McCardill. Clicking the link to the image entry tells us that the application was received on 4 April 1917, but that the details supplied by Mary were not enough to locate her in the 1851 census as requested. This does not necessarily mean that she did not receive a pension – simply that the evidence she requested to prove her age could not be found from the 1851 census.

Searches can be constructed in many ways to look for those who were living in the city when making an application, but also for those who may have been originally from the city and who had since moved away.

Additional documents from the application process, known as Form 37s, are also held at PRONI, catalogued under T550/2-37 (some are also available on microfilm under MIC/15A), with the records bound within set volumes for individual baronies (p.15). Whilst there is an available index of sorts to these records on microfilm, this will simply tell you whether there is an entry for a particular person – the remaining information on the index unfortunately does not correspond with the way that the records are compiled by PRONI within the registers (the index was drawn up by the Church of Jesus Christ of Latter-day Saints). You will therefore need to order up the relevant barony register for the area where your ancestor lived, and work your way through it one page at a time until the entry of interest is found.

The following are the relevant catalogue entries for Belfast:

- T550/3   Antrim Co., Belfast & Carrickfergus Baronies (1908–1922)
- T550/10   Antrim Co., Mixed Baronies (1908–1922)
- T550/18   Down Co., Castlereagh & Dufferin Baronies (1908–1922)
- T550/20   Down Co., Mixed Baronies. (1908–1922)

There were many successful and unsuccessful applicants from Belfast, but as with the NAI-held records, you may well find that a great deal of information can be found within these records whether or not a census entry was located for an applicant. The following case study shows their value:

Case study: My three times great-grandfather, Arthur Taylor, was born in Belfast in 1848, and made a series of applications for a search of the 1851 census between 14 February and 6 May 1918. He stated in his initial application that he had lived as a child at Abbey Street near Peter's Hill with his parents Arthur Taylor and Isabella Hall. This first search was duly carried out by the Public Record Office in Dublin, but he could not be located at that address.

Undeterred, he asked for another search, stating that as a child he had also lived for a time with his grandfather, named as Arthur Taylor, at a place that was either called McLelland's Lane, McLelland's Entry, or possibly Lime Street – as a child at the time his memory had obviously been quite vague. Again, the authorities carried out a search, and discovered that there was indeed an Arthur Taylor located there with his wife Ann, noting that they had married in 1819 (as recorded in the original census) – but once again there was no sign of Arthur Taylor, the applicant. Still undaunted, Arthur made a third attempt, suggesting that he had also lived as a child at both Cargill Street and Cargill Court. Once again, the authorities found no trace of him.

Whilst the fact that Arthur could not be found in the 1851 census was a blow, the very process of trying to find him led to me discovering several addresses where he claimed to have lived as a child in the late 1840s and early 1850s, as well as the names of his grandparents, the year in which they had married, and the part of Belfast in which they had resided.

TIP: It is not always obvious which census an extract has been requested from. But the age of the applicant, and the year of the application, usually stamped on the paperwork, should allow you to work it out in most cases.

Ulster Covenant and Declaration of Loyalty

The 'Ulster Covenant' was signed on 28 September 1912 by 237,368 Protestant men from the province of Ulster, as a protest against Home Rule for Ireland (p.11), whilst 234,046 women signed a parallel 'Declaration of Loyalty' in support of the campaign. In the centre of Belfast, the main place to sign the Covenant was City Hall, whilst women signed the Declaration at the Ulster Hall.

The round table on which the Ulster Covenant was signed in 1912 at City Hall, where it is now on display.

PRONI's 'Ulster Covenant' database allows you to search the documents by surname, forename, address, parliamentary division, district, place of signing, and even by the name of the agent gathering the signatures at each location. Signatures were gathered within districts within the parliamentary divisions of Belfast East (Pottinger, Victoria, Ormeau, Belfast, and Dock), Belfast North (West, Clifton, Ligoniel, Duncairn, Shankill, Fortwilliam, and St Anne's; also 'Not Recorded'), Belfast West (Shankill, Woodvale, West, Smithfield, and Falls), and Belfast South (St George's, Cromac, Windsor, and St Anne's; also 'Not Recorded'). Additional signatures are found under Antrim East and Belfast North (Greencastle and Whitehouse).

Although many people who had left Belfast and Ireland returned to Ulster to sign the Covenant, others signed it instead in locations much further away, including 2,000 who did so in Dublin, and many more who did so in overseas countries such as Scotland, England, the United States of America, Canada, and Australia.

> **TIP:** In most cases, signatories beyond Ulster gave their parish or home address back in Ireland, rather than the address of the place where they had settled.

An unusual example of just how far away some Belfast folk were when they signed it can be found on the database by selecting 'China' under the 'Place of Signing' menu option, for which nine names are returned, six of them from Belfast folk.

- John Ayre, 3 Harland Street, Ballymacrett [*sic*], Belfast
- George Richard Bellis, 15 Memel Street, Bridge End, Belfast
- John Bleakely, 235 Olive Terrace, Oldpark Road, Belfast
- James Marchall Boyd, 66 From Street, Ballymacarett, Belfast
- Frederick Ferguson, 80 Bankmore Street, Belfast
- Robert Meharg, 701 Greenville Avenue, Bloomfield, Belfast

All were serving on board the Royal Navy armoured cruiser HMS *Monmouth*, and signed it at Nanking (Nanjing).

Note that a person's signature can be a valuable research aid, as shown by the following example.

Case study: In the introduction to this book, I mentioned that my great great-grandfather Edwin Graham had signed the Ulster Covenant at Mountcollyer Street, Belfast (p.xii).

A few years later, just after the First World War, Edwin briefly left Belfast to work at Bootle, near Liverpool, England. His son John had served with the army, and a possible service record return found for him on Ancestry (p.149) failed to note the names of his parents.

However, included within the many papers was a letter written by Edwin to the British Army to explain that he was happy to receive the medals on his son's behalf, as John was 'at sea'. At the end of the letter, he signed his name – with the signature exactly matching that of his name on the Ulster Covenant, proving this to be the correct Edwin and John.

As well as accessing such information online, visitors to the City Hall Visitor Exhibition at Belfast City Hall can also search the returns on a computer there. In addition, the original round table on which the Union flag was placed can be seen, on which the document was signed by the Ulster Unionist leadership of the time.

1939 National Identity Register

No regular census was carried out in the UK in 1941, because of the Second World War, but on 29 September 1939 an emergency census

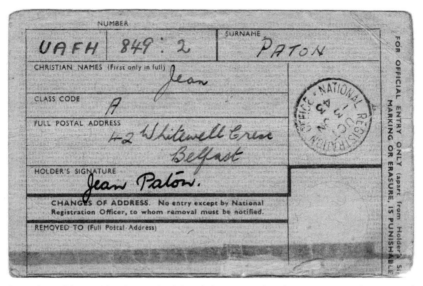

Second World War identity card of the author's grandmother Jean Paton (née Currie), issued to her after she signed the 1939 National Identity Register.

was carried out by the British Government for the purposes of issuing identity cards and a possible personnel draft. As a continuing member of the UK, Northern Ireland was included within this vast exercise, and its records have survived and are held at PRONI. They are accessible to view because no formal closure period has been imposed upon them, as

Case study: A few years ago, I made an application concerning my grandfather Charles Paton at his house at Whitewell Crescent in the Greencastle area of Belfast. To facilitate the request, I had to supply his address in 1939 and to provide PRONI with a scanned copy of his death certificate.

The details contained were limited, but in my case were extremely useful. I received my grandfather's name, his occupation and date of birth. He was listed as a branch manager at this point, confirming why he had moved from Scotland to Belfast just three years before (for the same firm), but crucially he was also described as having been born in 1905. Although Charles Paton eventually died in Donaghadee in 1989, he had actually been born in Belgium to Scottish parents, but the information I had previously sourced on his birth from other sources was both vague and conflicting. This date, however, was given by Charles himself – and on the basis of this record I was finally able to locate a baptismal record for him in Belgium.

with the decennial censuses, for they were never officially categorised as a census when the emergency legislation was passed for their creation.

The Northern Irish returns are the only such records within the UK for which you do not yet have to pay a fee. To access them you need to make a request to PRONI, through the archive's enquiry service. Information is only provided for those enumerated who are now deceased, for whom data protection laws no longer apply.

Street directories

Street directories can offer a very helpful substitute to help plug the gaps before, after, and in between the censuses in 1901 and 1911. They can name individuals (heads of households) at their street address, but also list them in occupational categories.

PRONI's 'Street Directories' covers 1819–1900, with twenty-seven volumes that can assist, but this does of course mean that there are gaps in the coverage. Specifically for Belfast are the following:

- Bradshaw's General and Commercial Directory 1819
- Belfast Directory 1831–32
- Matier's Belfast Directory 1835–36, 1939, and 1841–42
- Martin's Belfast Directory 1842–43
- Henderson's New Belfast and Northern Repository 1843–44
- Henderson's Belfast Directory and Northern Repository 1846–47, 1850, 1852
- The Belfast and Province of Ulster Directory 1852, 1858–59, 1863–64, 1865, 1866, 1870, 1877, 1880, 1884, 1887, 1890, 1892, 1895–97, 1899 and 1900

The database is not the easiest to use, but you can search by keyword (name or address), select a specific publication, or search over a broader year range. In some cases, you may find more than one entry for an individual in the same directory, perhaps listed at an address and in the separate occupations' listings. The original volumes are also available for consultation in the on-site Search Room.

Two other major collections of Belfast street directories are available online. The North of Ireland Family History Society's collection of Belfast directories is now available on Findmypast (p.47) as the 'Ireland, Belfast & Ulster Directories' database. This includes:

- The Belfast and Province of Ulster Directory 1890, 1900, 1904, 1912 and 1920

- The Belfast and Ulster Directory 1923–26, 1928, 1931–32, 1935–38, and 1942–48.

Findmypast also hosts Matier's Belfast Directory 1835–36 and Henderson's Belfast Directory from 1850.

Ulster Ancestry (**www.ulsterancestry.com**) hosts transcribed Belfast directories from 1800, 1806, 1807, and 1817, found in the County Antrim section.

The wonderful Lennon Wylie platform (**www.lennonwylie.co.uk**) hosts a substantial free-to-access collection of Belfast directories, covering 1805–1808, 1819, 1843, 1852, 1861, 1868, 1877, 1880, 1890, 1894, 1901, 1907–1910, 1912, 1918, 1924, 1932, 1939, 1943, 1947, 1951, 1955 and 1960. At the time of writing, the volumes up to 1924 were completely transcribed, with the later volumes having the main streets of Belfast transcribed, but not information on other town and counties in the volumes. The site also hosts information from the 1903–1904 and 1913 Telephone Directory for Belfast, as well as pages for Belfast from Pigot's directories in 1824. Some additional records are available at **www.lennonwylie.co.uk/ assortedstreets.htm**.

> **TIP:** The LennonWylie site offers a search box on its page using Google as the search engine. This can be unwieldy – I find it easier to choose a year's volume, and then search for a term using 'Control F' on my PC, or by simply browsing.

Note that in some cases individuals may well have relocated by the time that the directories were published.

Electoral records

The various surviving electoral registers for Belfast can help to not only determine the presence of a relative or ancestor in the town at a particular time but also to provide some useful family history clues about their status. From the twentieth century, when the franchise was substantially extended, it can be possible to determine when ancestors may have disappeared from the roll, which may offer potential clues to resettlement, emigration, or even death. However, the qualification to appear on such registers has changed dramatically across the centuries, starting with a very small pool indeed from the town's earliest days.

From its establishment as a corporation borough in 1613, there were regular elections held amongst Belfast's freemen, the twelve burgesses and the annually elected sovereign (mayor) to determine who would represent them as their MPs at the Irish Parliament in Dublin, until its abolition at the end of 1800. In the early eighteenth century, following the 1704 Act to Prevent the Further Growth of Popery, which also discriminated against the town's substantial Scottish Presbyterian community, the freemen were removed from the right to vote, with subsequent elections officially decided by the sovereign and burgesses alone. In truth, the appointees were effectively chosen by the Chichester family in what was essentially a 'rotten borough'.

Following Ireland's entry to the United Kingdom in 1801, the Corporation was able to send a single MP to the British Parliament. In 1832, the system was radically overhauled by the Representation of the People (Ireland) Act, when the town's electorate extended overnight from thirteen to over 1,600, with the vote now granted to those who held property with an annual rateable value of £10; leaseholders for lives; or those holding leases of at least sixty years. In addition, a second MP could now be voted for to represent the town's interests at Westminster.

The property qualifications to vote were finally abandoned by the Representation of the People Acts of 1918 and 1920, with the franchise extended to men over 21 and women over 30 (if they were university graduates in the constituency, or occupied a property with an annual rateable value of £5).

Following Partition in 1921, registered voters in Belfast had the right to vote in the election to the Northern Irish Parliament from 1921 to 1969. The first two elections in 1921 and 1925 were based on proportional representation, before switching to a first-past-the-post system in 1929, with the exception of Queen's University Belfast, which continued to operate a proportional system up to 1969. In 1968, the Electoral Law Act (Northern Ireland) Act changed the franchise again, now granting the right to vote to all men and women over the age of 18, with no property qualification required.

As well as choosing local councillors, from 1972 onwards Belfast's citizens have been able to vote for a series of assemblies, which continues to this day with the current Northern Irish Assembly at Stormont, as well as for the UK Parliament, and, from 1979 to 2019, the European Parliament.

There is no single repository that holds copies of all of Belfast's electoral rolls. The names of freemen from 1635 to 1796 are available in the *Town Book of the Corporation of Belfast* (Young, 2008), as are the names of burgesses appointed between 1613 and 1800 to act as MPs, and the city's sovereigns from 1613 to 1815. The Ulster Historical Foundation has an interesting article on Belfast's role in this period at **www. ancestryireland.com/history-of-the-irish-parliament/constituencies/ belfast/**, along with a searchable database of pre-1801 Irish MPs at **www. ancestryireland.com/family-records/biographies-of-the-members-of- the-irish-parliament/**, including entries for those representing Belfast.

The PRONI website's free-to-access 'Freeholders records' collection includes two searchable lists of voters for Belfast from 1837 (sourced from D/2966/5/1 and T/516), and a poll book for the city from 1832 to 1837 (from D/2472/1). These can be searched by name and street address, or the books can be browsed a page at a time; in some cases, genealogical information such as whether the elector has died since registering as a voter is noted, as well as instances of people moving to other districts. In addition to these names, you will also find landowners listed as holding freeholds elsewhere in Ulster within the database, but who were based in Belfast. For example, in four records from 1828 and 1832, a James Boomer is noted as having held land at the townland of Maymacullen in Co. Armagh, but as being resident in Belfast, although no specific address is given as to where he was based in the town. The same collection can also be searched on MyHeritage's 'Ireland, Ulster Freeholders' collection.

Registers of electors from Belfast from 1855 and 1876 are available at PRONI catalogued under BELF/5/1/1//1-2.

Belfast Central Library holds printed volumes of electoral registers for a small number of Belfast wards from 1939, and then a complete collection for the city from 1946 to 2007. More recent records are held by the Electoral Office of Northern Ireland (**www.eoni.org.uk**), although there are very strict rules to access these because of data protection legislation.

The British Library has copies of electoral registers for Belfast for the year 1937, and from 1947 onwards, catalogued as follows:

East Belfast	SPR.Mic.P.100/BL.I.B.1 (1937);
	BL.I.B.1 (1947–83);
	BL.I.B.6 (1984–95);
	BL.I.B.10 (from 1996)
North Belfast	SPR.Mic.P.101/BL.I.B.2 (1937);
	BL.I.B.2 (1947–83);
	BL.I.B.7 (1984–95);
	BL.I.B.11 (from 1996)
South Belfast	SPR.Mic.P.102/BL.I.B.3 (1937);
	BL.I.B.3 (1947–83);

	BL.I.B.8 (1984–95);
	BL.I.B.12 (from 1996)
West Belfast	SPR.Mic.P.103/BL.I.B.4 (1937);
	BL.I.B.4(1947–83);
	BL.I.B.9 (1984–95);
	BL.I.B.13 (from 1996)

PRONI also holds electoral registers from 1972 to 2001, created through the Electoral Office for Northern Ireland, and collated as the Chief Electoral Office archive. An information leaflet is available at **www. nidirect.gov.uk/publications/chief-electoral-office-records**.

Dissenters petitions

Within the Name Search database on the PRONI website are the '1775 Dissenters Petitions' from Counties Antrim and Down, with 191 names of people signing themselves as being from Belfast, who protested against an Irish Parliament law banning Presbyterians from attending Church of Ireland vestry meetings, a law which was later repealed as a consequence.

The original petitions have not survived, only transcripts recorded by genealogist Tenison Groves before the destruction of the Public Record Office in Dublin in 1922. These are catalogued by PRONI under T808/15307, and are included within PRONI's 'Name Search' database (p.27).

Maps

The PRONI website's free-to-access 'Historical Maps viewer' is a fun tool which allows you to see five historical Ordnance Survey maps for the north of Ireland, from 1832 to 1963, as well as two later twentieth-century maps, as follows:

- Edition 1 (1832 to 1846)
- Edition 2 (1846 to 1862)
- Edition 3 (1900 to 1907)
- Edition 4 (1905 to 1957)
- Edition 5 (1919 to 1963)
- 6-inch Irish Grid (1952 to 1969)
- 1:10,000 metric Irish Grid (1957 to 1986)

Before using the site for the first time, it is worth taking the 'Map Viewer Tour' of the various tools and functions available – this is as accessible on the map's display screen by clicking on the icon that looks like a crumpled map in the top right corner, on the main menu bar.

Using the search box on this site you can search for an area by townland, parish or town/city name, or with a modern postcode.

Case study: A useful example to show the growth of the city is to search for the postcode of PRONI, being BT3 9HQ. In the first and second edition maps, you will be hard pressed to find any buildings, as the area occupied by the archive today was on land still to be reclaimed from Belfast Lough at the time!

The third edition map, however, from 1900 to 1907, shows a dramatic change to the landscape, with the same area now shown to be on what was once Abercorn Road, next to the Abercorn Basin, in the city's docks areas.

By the fourth edition, Abercorn Road is no more, replaced by huge shipbuilding works. By unclicking all the historical maps options, the default modern map will show the outline of the PRONI building today, located on Titanic Boulevard.

TIP: Being at a 6 inch to the mile scale, the earlier maps for Belfast are quite basic, but via the widget tools at the top right of the search screen, you can also overlay a series of 'layers' on to the city map, including points of interest (such as courts, churches and schools) and boundary information for its townlands. It is also possible to 'swipe' between two maps at the same location, to give you an instant then and now comparison.

Two great published resources for exploring the development of the city across time are available from the Royal Irish Academy (**www.ria.ie**) – *Irish Historic Towns Atlas no. 12: Belfast, part I, to 1840* by Raymond Gillespie and Stephen A. Royle (2003) and *Irish Historic Towns Atlas no. 17: Belfast, part II, 1840 to 1900* by Stephen A. Royle (2007). Incomplete online editions are available at **www.ria.ie/irish-historic-towns-atlas-online-belfast-part-i-1840** and **www.ria.ie/irish-historic-towns-atlas-online-belfast-part-ii-1840-1900**. In particular, the 'Text' documents online include detailed lists of all the streets to have come and gone in the city, as well as lists of institutions such as schools, churches, industrial facilities and more. Only a small sample of the maps is available online, with a substantial expansion available in the print editions.

Valuation records

The tithe applotment records (p.28) from the 1820s-1840s can help to locate some Belfast landowners and holdings in the early to mid 19th century, but for the city in the 1860s, the Tenement Valuation of Ireland, can be especially useful. Carried out by boundary commissioner Richard Griffith, the records were published as the 'Primary Valuation of Ireland', but are today better known as 'Griffith's Valuation'.

A very helpful platform offering access is that at AskAboutIreland.ie (**www.askaboutireland.ie**). This site is not only free it also offers copies of Ordnance Survey maps, albeit not quite contemporary (they were used for subsequent valuation revisions), which in most cases can be used to plot the locations of all the properties recorded, with individual lot numbers marked out with red boundaries. Searches on the site can be carried out by surname, forename, county, barony, union or parish, but not by townland. For the 'Union' category, you will need to select either 'Belfast' or 'Belfast (Part of)' after choosing either County Antrim or County Down from the relevant drop-down menu.

The results page allows you to see a brief summary of the items returned for the search, and clicking on the 'Details' link will provide additional information such as the townland and street name, the landlord's details, and the all-important publication date.

The AskAboutIreland platform hosts a free-to-access version of Griffith's Valuation.

TIP: AskAboutIreland can be a little glitchy. If after viewing a record you try to carry out a second search, you may find that the options to focus on an area using the barony, union and parish fields will not work. You may need to come out of the site altogether and go back in.

Let's target a possible record for my three times great-grandfather, Arthur Taylor, who was a sawyer. I know from the Belfast Street directories that Arthur had moved to 16 Cargill Street by 1856, where he remained until the early 1860s. A search for him on AskAboutIreland.ie using the terms 'Antrim' for the county, 'Belfast' for the union, and 'Shankill' as the parish, produces three results. I quickly establish that the first is the correct one, with the 'Details' summary page confirming his address at 'Cargill Street, Upper', and the record published in 1860. By selecting the 'Original Page' I can see the published return, which notes the following:

No. and Letters of Reference to Map.	Names.		Description of Tenement	Area	Rateable Annual Valuation		Total Annual Valuation of Rateable Property
	Streets, &c, & Occupiers	Immediate Lessors			Land.	Buildings.	
	Upper Cargill Street *(Ord. S. 20)*			A. R. P.	£. s. d.	£. s. d.	£. s. d.
16	Arthur Taylor	Alexander Green	House and yard			3. 0. 0.	3. 0. 0

The new information here is the name of Arthur's landlord and the amount of annual rent he was subjected to. However, if I had no idea where Arthur lived in Belfast at this point, the search has revealed three possibilities that I can explore further.

TIP: If you need to search by townland, or are having difficulties with a search, alternative presentations of the collection are available on Findmypast's 'Griffith's Valuation 1847–1864' database, and on Ancestry's 'Ireland, Griffith's Valuation, 1847–1864' collection.

Valuation revision books

Following Griffith's Valuation, a series of 'valuation revision books' can be freely consulted on the PRONI website at **www.nidirect.gov.uk/services/searching-valuation-revision-books**, which can detail changes of occupancy and ownership of properties up to circa 1930. The database is not name searchable, but can be searched by townland or street name to locate the relevant register.

Let's take the example of my three times great-grandfather Thomas Graham. I know from vital records events for his children and contemporary street directories that he was living at 86 Henry Street from at least March 1862 until his address changed to 92 Henry Street in 1870, before eventually settling at 206 York Street for several more years from November 1871 until 1881.

If I visit the revision books' database and search for the term 'Henry Street', several registers are listed, but the following is the correct entry for the period:

PLACE NAME	URBAN	TOWNLAND	PARISH	COUNTY	DATE FROM	DATE TO	PRONI REFERENCE
Henry Street	Belfast, City of	Townparks	Shankill	Antrim	1862	1881	VAL/12/B/43/B/2

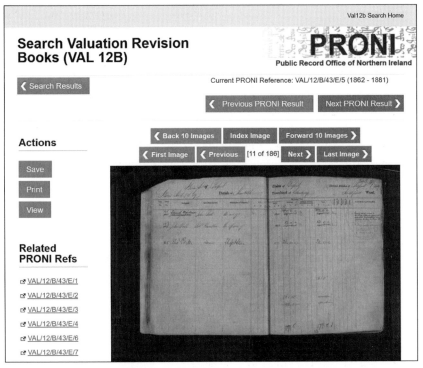

Changes to property holdings recorded after Griffith's Valuation can be found via PRONI's Valuation Revision Books database.

By clicking on the hyperlink for the PRONI reference, I am taken to a page showing me the digitised register. Clicking on the green button marked 'Index Image' takes me to page listing all the streets in the volume, and the page numbers where their entries can be found. In this case there are two page numbers noted, a scored out '296' in black, and a replacement in red ink, '303' (the pages have been renumbered at some point). I can now move forward a page at a time, or ten pages at a time, until I eventually find Henry Street.

Once located, I work my way forwards a few more pages until I identify the entry for 86 Henry Street. As with the page numbers, I soon discover that the house numbers have been renumbered also, with the original house numbers in pencil, and scored out with a new number written in red on top. In this case, the pencilled number '86' is replaced with a red inked '92', telling me that Thomas never in fact moved between 86 and 92 Henry Street, his house was simply renumbered. Additional information given includes the fact that he was paying rent to a Richard Gordon, at an annual rate of £6 10s.

The record also shows that the previous occupant was a Hugh Heron, with his named scored out and replaced by that of Thomas. Unfortunately, in this case it does not tell me when this happened, but usually in the books you will see the year given in the far right-hand column, written in the same colour of ink as the recorded correction.

The Registry of Deeds

The Registry of Deeds is one of the most important family history resources for pre-civil registration Irish research. It was created in 1708 as a means to help Protestants adhering to the Church of Ireland to voluntarily register title to their lands, although lands with leases shorter than twenty-two years could not be registered until late in the eighteenth century. By the late eighteenth century and the early nineteenth century, Presbyterians and Roman Catholics became better represented within the Registry's pages following the relaxation of the Penal Laws and the improvements in access to property ownership. Amongst the many transactions that the Registry holds are details of deeds conveying interests in properties from transactions such as sales, mortgages, leases, marriage settlements, and wills.

The registration system introduced was fairly straightforward. A deed concerning a property transaction would be signed by both parties to the agreement, and then witnessed. An abridged copy was created, called a 'memorial', with indentured copies provided to both parties.

The transaction was then recorded into the registers held in Dublin, and the original memorials filed away for safekeeping.

There are two main indexes for searching the Registry: the Townlands Index and the Grantors Index. Whichever you choose to use, you need to locate the relevant entry, note down the Transcript Book volume number, the page number and the number of the relevant memorial, before you can consult the original entry for the deed of interest. The Townlands Index notes deeds under the names of the townlands in which a property is located. From 1708 to 1828 it is arranged by county, with each volume arranging townlands in alphabetical sections, whereas from 1828, the county volumes are further divided by baronies (p.15), with separate indexes for cities and counties corporate, including Belfast.

The main historical series of registers prior to Partition is held at the Registry of Deeds offices in Dublin, as part of the Property Registration Authority, with copies available on microfilm at PRONI from 1708 to 1929. PRONI also has paper indexes from 1923 to 1989 for Northern Irish registered entries post-Partition.

TIP: A twenty-seven-page guide on the history of the Registry of Deeds is available from the PRA at **www.tailte.ie/wp-content/uploads/2022/10/Introduction-to-the-Memorials-and-Transcription-Books-at-the-Registry-of-Deeds.pdf**

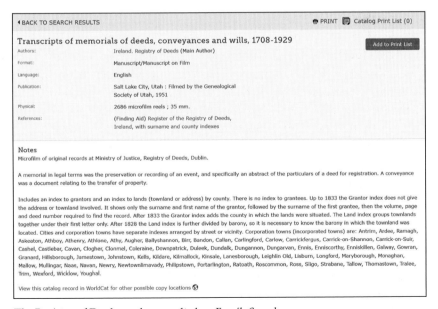

The Registry of Deeds can be consulted on FamilySearch.

The majority of the more historical records on microfilm have been digitised and made available through the FamilySearch catalogue at **https://familysearch.org/search/catalog/185720**. This hosts all the relevant microfilms, including Grantors Indexes (Names Indexes) arranged in alphabetical order, and within concurrent chronological periods, followed by Land Indexes (Townlands Indexes) arranged in a similar order. The microfilms for the deeds themselves are the final records catalogued on the page, arranged both chronologically and by volume number.

If I want to search for a person called James Carruthers in Belfast in the early to mid-1830s, who I believe had a connection to Berry Street in the city, I would be as well to start with the Land Index, which has Belfast's streets arranged in alphabetical order (albeit with street name entries for each letter of the alphabet not listed in alphabetical order within that letter's category!). Scrolling through the list of microfilms I see one entitled 'Land index: Armagh, Carlow, Cavan; cities of Belfast, Cork, Drogheda, Kilkenny, Limerick, Londonderry 1833–1835'. Clicking on the camera icon beside this takes me through.

The street listings for the city of Belfast start on page 341 of the digital microfilm. Just two pages in, on page 343, I find an entry for Berry Street as follows:

Lands	Parish	Grantors	Grantees	Year of Registry	No. of Fyle and Volume of Transcript and Abstract Books	No. of Memorial and Page of Transcript Book	Page of Day Book
Berry Street	Belfast	O'Brien, John	Carruthers, James	1833	4	151	78

The index tells me that I need to look up page 78 of the fourth volume for 1833, for memorial number 151.

Returning to the list of microfilms on Family Search, the year 1833 and volume 4 are covered by the film indexed as 'Deeds, etc., v. 3–5 1833'. Clicking on the camera icon again, I now locate the fourth volume, and after locating the start of the fourth volume, I eventually find the record on page 257 of the film (see **https://bit.ly/1833deedexample**). On reading this I learn that the memorial document concerns a mortgage taken out on 1 March 1833 by James Carruthers of Galvally, County Down, from John O'Brien, a Belfast woollen draper, to the value of £200, for a farm property at Ballyhackamore townland previously owned by a James O'Linn, as well as a piece of land on the south side of Berry Street in Belfast, previously owned by a David Goodlaw.

As James Carruthers is listed as the grantee of the transaction, he will not appear in the Grantors Index for this transaction (there would be an entry for John O'Brien). However, he may well be listed in other records in that role, and so a search of the Grantors Index for him should not be ruled out.

> **TIP:** Whilst there is no separate index to grantees, this is something that the ongoing volunteer-based Registry of Deeds Index Project Ireland at **https://irishdeedsindex.net** is currently addressing, offering a further way to try to locate entries of interest.

The Land Registry

The Land Registry was introduced in Ireland in 1892 as a means to provide a more flexible title registration system than the Registry of Deeds could offer. Following Partition, a separate Land Registry continued in Northern Ireland, in parallel to the Registry of Deeds.

Today these are both managed by Land and Property Services (p.40), which operates five customer services, including one in Belfast. In 1951, a Statutory Charge Register was also established, for purchasers to be able to check in advance the existence of any restrictions concerning a property prior to purchase.

Further information on access to the Registry of Deeds and Land Registry services is available on the LPS site at **www.nidirect.gov.uk/information-and-services/buying-your-home/land-and-property-registers**.

Irish Land Commission

Following the Famine and the subsequent Land War in Ireland, a new Irish Land Commission was established from 1881. Amongst its roles was that of a tenancy purchasing commission, assisting those wishing to buy their holdings outright with loans to be repaid over thirty-five years at 5 per cent interest, and granting tenants *vesting orders* for their new holdings; essentially title deeds in their name, clear of any previous burdens or encumbrances. The scheme was further extended in 1885, 1889, 1903, and 1909.

The Land Commission files contain a great deal of supporting material for property sales, including title deeds, copies of wills, estate plans and considerably more, which landowners were required to submit to establish initial proof of ownership prior to a sale. Following Partition, the Commission's historical files were divided into those for Northern Ireland and those for the new Free State. The body in the north was renamed the Land Purchase Commission (NI), and its work continued until it was finally disbanded on 1 April 1937, at which point the records were transferred to PRONI, where they can be accessed under LR1 and LR2.

Further guidance on the background to the records, and their use, is available from PRONI in its information leaflet, *Your Family Tree: Land Registry*, accessible at **www.nidirect.gov.uk/publications/family-tree-land-registry-records**.

> **TIP:** For a much more detailed examination of the background to the tithe records, the various valuation records, the Registry of Deeds, and the Land Commission records, consult my book *Tracing Your Irish Ancestors Through Land Records* (2021, Pen and Sword).

Probate records

When a person has passed away, it is possible for their estate to be administered in the courts through the probate process, with the express wishes of the deceased recorded in a will taken into account. The court issues a 'grant of probate' in such cases to an executor, or executors, to carry out the deceased's wishes as expressed in a will. Where a will has not been left, the deceased's estate can still be taken through the courts, after an inventory has been compiled of his or her assets, and an executor or executors again appointed to sort out any debts or to collect any money owed. In such cases, the document issued is a 'letter of administration' or 'admon'. Today, the probate process in Belfast is handled by the High Court of Justice (**www.nidirect.gov.uk/articles/probate**).

Prior to 1858, the ecclesiastical courts of the Church of Ireland handled probate cases. With the disestablishment of the church from January 1871, its records were all handed in to the Public Record Office in Dublin, and were thus sadly destroyed in the Civil War in 1922, with only indexes surviving, and copies of wills and letters of administration which survived elsewhere. Many names for those whose estates went through the process are included within the PRONI Name Search database (p.27), within the 'Pre-1858 Wills and Admons' dataset. This includes 4,890 names of Belfast folk who were recorded as having a will probated by the ecclesiastical courts before 1858, with a further seventy-three names returned for a search for the parish of 'Shankill'. In most cases, you may simply see an index entry naming a person, with their address given as

'Belfast', and the year of death noted, although you may be lucky to find an extra detail or two included – a search for Maria Adair, for example, notes that she was from Belfast, with probate granted in 1846, but with her date of death also given as 28 September 1846.

If you are extremely lucky, you may win the genealogical lottery and find that a copy of a document destroyed in Dublin has popped up elsewhere, and has been deposited at PRONI. In such cases the entry will also give you the reference number, which can be used to retrieve the document.

After 1858 the situation improves somewhat. A new civil court-based Principal Probate Registry was established in Dublin, as well as a network of District Probate Registries across the country, one of which was based at Belfast, which obviously covers the city area. An annual *Calendar of Grants of Probate of Wills and Letters of Administration made in the Principal Registry and its District Registries* was also established in 1858, providing published summaries of the value of estates to go through the courts, the names of the deceased, their executors, whether they were testate (i.e. whether they left a will) or intestate, and where the probate case was heard.

PRONI's Will Calendars database currently offers access to the records from the Belfast district registry from 1858 to 1965. The Belfast district probate registry heard some 291,827 cases in this period, although many of these were from beyond the city, within a wider catchment area in Counties Antrim and Down. The good news is that although the Belfast district records were destroyed in Dublin, copies held in the local registry office in Belfast survived, which PRONI has digitised and made freely available online for the period 1858–1909. The Calendar summaries also exist for the same period, and continue up to 1965 for the whole of Northern Ireland. At the time of writing, PRONI has plans to extend the collection further into the latter part of the twentieth century at some point in the near future.

TIP: Post-1965 calendar volumes covering Belfast and Northern Ireland can be consulted in PRONI's Search Room (p.24) , and original copies of the relevant wills ordered up for view.

The two other probate districts in the north were at Armagh (covering most of Armagh, Fermanagh, Tyrone, Louth and Monaghan) and Londonderry (covering Derry and Donegal, as well as a small part of Tyrone). Whilst these dealt with people's estates from their respective areas, executors and relatives from Belfast may have been named with their records, and so should not be ignored. Copies of district records for Armagh are available on the PRONI site from 1858 to 1918, and Londonderry from 1858 to 1899.

It is important to note that from 1858 Belfast folk could have their estate probated through the local district registry, or alternatively at the Principal Registry in Dublin. The calendar entries on PRONI's database from 1858 to 1921 are for the district probate registry only, and do not include any cases for Belfast folk which may have been heard in Dublin. However, digitised images from the original published calendars for this period can be searched and consulted via the NAI's records site at **www.genealogy. nationalarchives.ie**, in its 'Calendars of Wills and Administrations, 1858– 1922' database, although this only includes entries for folk from the north up to 1917. Although all records for the Principal Registry prior to 1904 have not survived, the calendars can at least offer some basic details.

> **TIP:** Don't forget to check newspapers (p.162) for possible probate announcements, including the *Belfast Gazette* (p.165).

A separate database on the NAI site can also help, entitled 'Will Registers 1858–1900' (**http://census.nationalarchives.ie/search/wr/home.jsp**). This database states that the district probate register for Belfast is held at PRONI, implying that the database only holds entries from the southern registries for the period, but some 965 entries for folk from Belfast are included – although some of these are duplicate entries within the database (with broken links accompanying them), and include returns for names of both executors and the deceased.

Many of these documents contain the same text as the documents found on the PRONI site, but in a different hand, and often more legible.

> **Case study:** Samuel Bill was a school teacher from Ashley Park, Belfast, who died on 16 February 1901.
>
> A search on the PRONI website not only shows his calendar entry, which shows that he died on 16 February, it also has a copy of the document, recorded on 31 August 1900, and details of the probate from 3 May 1901, as recorded by the district probate registry. When consulted, the handwriting has a very pronounced slant to the right, making it incredibly difficult to read without manipulating the image in some way.
>
> However, on the NAI website, a copy of Samuel's will is also included, which is much easier to read, although the details of the subsequent probate are not included.

Chapter 7

DAILY LIFE

Births, marriages and deaths can offer a beginning, middle and end to an ancestor's story, but there was a lot else that happened in a person's life in between.

In Chapter 8, I will look at some of the various occupations that dominated the working lives of our folk. In this chapter, I will first examine some of the other resources available that can be examined to find out more about their early lives, and how they got through the day when there were times of crisis, or when they crossed the line with what society deemed to be tolerable behaviour.

Gettin' learned – Education

Thanks to its heavy influx of Scots from the seventeenth century, Presbyterianism had a great influence on matters of education in Belfast. In Scotland, the Reformation settlement of 1560 led to a requirement for every parish to have a school established, with education and parochial discipline underpinning the Kirk's Calvinist drive to steer its parishioners towards 'Godliness'. As an educated flock could read the Bible, education became an absolute priority, a tenet of the Kirk's doctrine taken by its followers to Belfast.

Prior to the nineteenth century, the individual churches provided for their own schooling, with a boys' school established in 1762 by First Presbyterian Church on Rosemary Street. In 1786, the church's Rev. James Crombie established Belfast Academy (Belfast Royal Academy from 1888), as a high school and college for middle- to upper-class boys, initially situated on Academy Street, but from 1880 at a new sandstone structure on the Cliftonville Road. Girls were finally admitted to the upper school from 1900, albeit segregated from the boys, before a mixed education approach was established in 1923. A history of the BRA, as

A late nineteenth-century view of Belfast Royal Academy.

well as the names of notable alumni, can be found on its website at **www. belfastroyalacademy.com**, with published histories including *Belfast Royal Academy: The First Century 1785–1885* by A. T. Q. Stewart (1985), and *Belfast Royal Academy: The Second Century 1885–1985* by Edward McCamley (1996). The NIFHS has a copy of the BRA admissions register from 1880 to 1935.

In 1810, the Belfast Academical Institution was founded by Presbyterian reformers as a boarding school at College Square East, providing both a boys' school and a further education college department, with the latter's General Certificate recognised as the equivalent of a Scottish degree. In 1831 it became the Royal Belfast Academical Institution, although today it is more colloquially known as the 'Inst'. Many of those who studied at Inst's collegiate department went on to become Presbyterian ministers, whilst between 1835 and 1849 it was also possible to train at the body's very own medical college, the Royal Institution Hospital at Barrack Street. The development of Queen's College (later Queen's University Belfast), ended its collegiate programme. In the First World War, 132 of the school's alumni lost their lives; 213 were decorated for action, including one Victoria Cross. A history of the school is available on the school's website at **http://rbai.org.uk**, whilst an interesting account of its more radical origins can be read online at **https://en.wikipedia.org/ wiki/Royal_Belfast_Academical_Institution#Dissident_foundation**.

In 1913, the *Royal Belfast Academical Institution Centenary Volume 1810– 1910*, by Joseph R. Fisher and John H. Robb was published. The book's appendices included a list of students and scholars from 1814 to 1912, as well as a list of students who received a General Certificate in the Faculty of Arts from 1817 to 1838. Both are accessible via the members-only section of website of the Presbyterian Historical Society of Ireland (p.37), with an introduction to the Presbyterian connection to the Inst detailed on its website at **https://presbyterianhistoryireland.com/web-resources/minister-lists-fasti/royal-belfast-academical-institution/**. Following the merger in 1840 of the General Synod of Ulster and the Secession Synod to create the Presbyterian Church in Ireland, a new Presbyterian educational institute was established in 1853 as the Assembly's College, today known as Union Theological College, with a history of its evolution found at **www.union.ac.uk**. Robert Allen's *The Presbyterian College, Belfast, 1853–1953* (1954) also has a list of students, which can again be searched on the PHSI website.

In 1868, a similar institution for the provision of the Methodist church in the city, to train boys and ministers, opened as Methodist College on the Malone Road, with 141 pupils. Initially formed as a boys' school, just three months into its existence the decision was taken to teach girls also, it remaining a co-educational facility ever since. Today the college is more colloquially referred to today as 'Methody'. The school's website has a potted history available at **www.methody.org/about**, with its records held at PRONI under SCH/955.

The forerunner to Belfast High School, Pyper Academy, was first established in 1854 at Eglinton Street. After briefly being known also as Eglantine Academy, it soon changed its name to Belfast Mercantile Academy, and from 1874 was based at Glenravel Street. From 1929 it was referred to as 'Belfast Mercantile Academy High School for Boys and Girls (from 6 years of age and upwards)', eventually adopting the simpler name of 'Belfast High School' from 1 August 1942. The school now lies just beyond the outskirts of Belfast at Jordanstown.

In 1894, Campbell College was later established on the Belmont Estate by philanthropist Henry James Campbell, where it continues to provide education to students from across the world on its 100-acre woodland campus. 'The Campbell Story' at **www.campbellcollege.co.uk/welcome-to-campbell/the-campbell-story** names some of its alumni, and offers a tribute to former staff and students who lost their lives in the First World War through its 'Men Behind the Glass' project. A database of former students from 1892 to 1938 is accessible via Emerald Ancestors (p.51), whilst a register from 1954 is available on **www.lennonwylie.co.uk**.

Whilst the schools mentioned so far were primarily established for middle- to upper-class Protestant families to send their sons to, not everyone in Belfast society could afford to be educated in such illustrious surroundings, with the working classes seeking their learning from the church and from other entrepreneurial establishments. Belfast's first Sunday School was opened in 1802 and, following the success of the movement across the town, a more formal school was erected in 1811 at Frederick Street for the children of labourers, followed by the Brown Street Sunday School in 1814 in the Shankill, which became a day school from 1821, and later a National School (p.123). Its records can be consulted at Belfast Central Library (p.34). Elsewhere, a school for the blind had opened in 1801, initially holding lessons at an Independent Meeting House on Donegall Street (later at King Street), and then from a purpose-built facility at College Street from 1836.

For the education of young girls, Margaret Byers set up Ladies' Collegiate School in 1859 at 13 Wellington Place, which from 1888 became Victoria College (**www.victoriacollege.org.uk**). In 1924, the school moved to Cranmore Park, with its former building in Belfast's Lower Crescent now hosting the Crescent Arts Centre. In 1870, another boarding school for girls was set up by Anna Hunter at College Square, later moving to Princess Gardens, where from 1901 it became Princess Gardens School. In August 1887, the school merged with Ashleigh College to form the current all girls' grammar school at Hunterhouse College.

For the maintenance and education of destitute girls, a union school was first founded as far back as 1795. With the aid of prominent suffragist Isabella Tod, Byers later set up the Belfast Women's Temperance Association in 1874, which led in the 1880s to the establishment of the Shamrock Lodge Industrial School for destitute girls at Lagan Village (**www.childrenshomes.org.uk/BelfastVictoria/**), which later moved in 1892 to Ligoniel. Margaret Byers acted as its first superintendent for almost a quarter of a century.

With Byers' support, as well as from others, Tod was later successful in securing rights for girls to sit public exams through the 1878 Education (Ireland) Act, and to be granted degrees from the Royal University of Ireland through the 1879 Universities (Ireland) Act.

Following the extension of the English-based Industrial School system to Ireland in 1868, which educated juvenile offenders, St Patrick's Industrial School for Roman Catholic Boys (**www.childrenshomes. org.uk/BelfastStPatrickBoysIS/**) was set up on Donegall Street, as well as an equivalent school for girls on the Crumlin Road from 1869 (**www.childrenshomes.org.uk/BelfastStPatrickGirlsIS/**). An affiliated institution, Sacred Heart Industrial School for Girls, was later set up in Whiteabbey in 1896. Elsewhere, the Industrial School Ship 'Gibraltar' was established in Belfast Lough from 1872 to accommodate and train over 300 Protestant boys aged 10–14 (**www.childrenshomes.org.uk/ TSGibraltar/**), with younger boys aged under 10 instead sent to Fox Lodge Industrial School from 1884 onwards (**www.childrenshomes. org.uk/BelfastFoxIS/**). Hampton House Industrial School for Protestant Girls was set up at Balmoral in 1873 (see **www.childrenshomes.org.uk/ BelfastHamptonIS/**).

In November 1833, just four years after Catholic emancipation, St Malachy's College was established on the Antrim Road, opening with just ten day pupils and eight boarders. Today it retains the status of Ireland's oldest diocesan college, its motto being *Gloria ab Intus*, meaning 'glory from within'. The website of its alumni association at **www. stmalachysalumni.co.uk** notes proudly that 'We're exactly where we've always been!', and currently hosts historical class photographs from 1962 onwards.

The college was not the first Catholic school in Belfast, however, with that honour falling to St Patrick's National School on Donegall Street, which opened in 1828, and which taught pupils from the area until its eventual closure in 1982. The National Schools system was initially formally established from 1831 as means to set up non-denominational

St Patrick's National School, Donegall Street, first opened in 1828. From 186,7 the Christian Brothers established a Ragged School alongside the National School in the building.

primary level education across Ireland, run by a national Board of Education, and as a means to close down the more informal 'hedge schools' that had previously provided the only means of education for many within the Catholic community. According to the government's Chief Secretary, Edward Stanley, they were supposed to be 'admitting children of all religious persuasions, should not interfere with the peculiar tenets of any', but whilst some schools did have mixed classes, most soon became affiliated to one denomination or another. Whilst the system did make a huge improvement in functional literacy in the English language, it was deemed by many to be massively damaging to the ability of the Irish language to survive and flourish.

Whilst the earliest registers from Belfast's National Schools, which later evolved into the city's public elementary and then primary schools, have not survived, records from 1860s to the 1940s are held at PRONI. An index to its Schools Collection is available as a 101-page PDF document accessible at **www.nidirect.gov.uk/publications/index-school-collections**, which provides each school with a catalogue number, with which a search can be performed on the online catalogue.

If I take the example of Dee Street School at Knockbreda, I would scroll down to the list for Knockbreda, for which there are twenty-two entries, and locate the entry for Dee Street, which tells me that its records are available under SCH/636. However, if I now search the catalogue by typing in SCH/636, I get a single return that simply says 'Dee Street National School', which is only helpful in telling me that *something* is there!

Instead, I need to try to find how the records are subdivided under this collection. If I type in SCH/636/1, I get a slightly more fruitful return, with the site telling me that this catalogue number holds registers from 1901 to 1934. If I subdivide this further, and try SCH/636/1/1, I am told now that the records for this catalogue number are for a 'Register (male) [date of entrance August 1901–October 1917]', whilst SCH/636/1/2 is for a 'Register (female) [dates of entrance April 1903–September 1920]'. National Education Board grant applications for schools from 1832

TIP: Most children attended school locally. If you don't know which school your ancestor attended, a good starting point is to consult a contemporary Ordnance Survey map (p.107) to locate institutions close to the family home.

to 1889, catalogued under ED/1, have been digitised also, and can be accessed through the online catalogue.

Many other school records are held at PRONI, which can be sourced from the catalogue by simply typing in the name of the institution, and looking for returns with catalogue numbers beginning with 'SCH'. For example, a search for 'Methodist College' as an exact phrase returns eighty-five entries, but the records from the school itself will be those filed under SCH/955.

For more on PRONI's education records, read its online *Local History Guide: 5 National Education Records* and the *Ministry/Department of Education Archive* guide, whilst for additional resources on the education of young girls in Belfast consult the *Guide to Women's History* (p.113–118).

> **TIP:** A brilliant history of the Irish education system is found within Susan M. Parkes' book *A Guide to the Sources for the History of Irish Education 1780–1922* (2010, Four Courts Press).

Workhouses and the Poor Law

Over the centuries of its existence, in times of financial hardship Belfast people could seek assistance from various bodies. The Church of Ireland vestry was one such source that regularly provided financial assistance to members of the parish in times of need, for example with support payments to widows or to those who had fallen seriously ill. As the state church, the vestry did not just make such payments to those adhering to the Anglican faith but to anyone in the parish, irrespective of their denomination.

Unfortunately, the accessible or surviving vestry records for most of Belfast's churches at PRONI tend to start quite late in the nineteenth century, although the records for St Patrick's at Ballymacarrett date back to 1850, those for St Matthew's go back to 1858, whilst St Anne's vestry records survive from 1808. Full details are in the archive's 'Guide to Church Records' (p.68). Some additional Belfast records are also held at the Representative Church Body Library in Dublin, the earliest being for St Luke's from 1868. A guide to its holdings is available at **www.ireland. anglican.org/cmsfiles/pdf/AboutUs/library/vestrybooks.pdf**.

In addition to the assistance from the Church of Ireland, the kirk session records from the Presbyterian denominations are also worth consulting, for payments that may have been made to members of their congregations. Again, the PRONI guide can help to identify what is held there – for example, for All Souls (2nd) Non-Subscribing Presbyterian Church there is a series of poor accounts from 1792 to 1816 available.

Prior to the eighteenth century, an association existed in Belfast from as early as 1631 which provided some limited poor relief to its

Clifton House, home to the Belfast Charitable Society's Poor House from 1774.

members in the town. In 1752, the Belfast Charitable Society (see p.35) was established and, after a significant fundraising endeavour, opened a Poor House at Clifton House in 1774 to help with the distress of the town's most destitute inhabitants. The Society's Heritage Centre has several records dating back to the creation of the institution, including applications forms for those seeking relief, and admissions books detailing inhabitants from 1805 to 1882, which may name their next of kin, their religious denomination, their residential addresses, and when and how they were eventually discharged. A later series of books, from 1882 to 1972, also record those who were admitted to the society's Old Peoples' Home. For more on the collections available at Clifton House visit **https://cliftonbelfast.com/collections/**.

In 1809, a House of Industry was established at Smithfield, where those who were unemployed could be put to work manufacturing goods whilst being supported by voluntary donations from civil society, as well as from sums levied from those prosecuted by the Police Magistrate for behaviour such as drunkenness and rioting. To assist with local distress in 1826, a Ladies' Clothing Society was established, followed by the Society of the Relief of the Destitute Sick, formed by Francis Spalding Esq. of Edinburgh.

The implementation of the 1838 Poor Relief (Ireland) Act led to a massive overhaul of the state's poor law system. The newly established poor law union of Belfast from June 1839 was served by a new workhouse which opened its doors from 1 January 1841. During the Famine, additional capacity was added, and from January 1847 a new fever hospital was erected. An informative article summarising the history of the workhouse, which was located at 51 Lisburn Road, can be found on Peter Higginbotham's excellent Workhouses site at **www.workhouses. org.uk/Belfast/**.

> **TIP:** PRONI's *The Great Irish Famine* guide at **https://www.nidirect. gov.uk/publications/great-irish-famine** may help with resources to help with Famine research.

The records of the Belfast Board of Guardians from 1842 to 1951, which was responsible for overseeing the workhouse and the poor relief system, are held at PRONI under BG/7. The archive's guide to its Poor Law Records is available at **www.nidirect.gov.uk/publications/family-tree-poor-law-records**. Through its online catalogue, PRONI has also made available the indexes to the admission registers from 1892 to 1921. These can be searched as follows:

i) On the catalogue search page type in the relevant code within the 'PRONI Ref:' box for a period of interest, for example BG/7/ GK/1, which calls up entries for the first available register, covering July–October 1892.

ii) After you click Search, one entry appears in the results, with at the far right-hand side the word 'View' presented as a blue hyperlink. Once you click on this you will be asked to agree to a copyright declaration – click on 'I Agree'. You will then be asked if you wish to save the file or open it with a PDF viewer, and can then view the document.

The registers list applicants in alphabetical order of surname (although not in strict order under each individual letter) for the period in question. The information provided is the individual's number in the workhouse register, the pauper's name, and their age. Once an entry is found, you will then be able to look for the original record at PRONI itself.

The following PRONI codes should help you to focus on the relevant periods of time within the indexes:

BG/7/GK/1 Jul 1892–Oct 1892	BG/7/GK/37 Oct 1903–Jan 1904	BG/7/GK/73 Apr 1912–Jul 1912
BG/7/GK/2 Dec 1893–Mar 1894	BG/7/GK/38 Jan 1904–May 1904	BG/7/GK/74 Jul 1912–Oct 1912
BG/7/GK/3 Apr 1894–Jul 1894	BG/7/GK/39 May 1904–Aug 1904	BG/7/GK/75 Oct 1912–Dec 1912
BG/7/GK/4 Jul 1894–Oct 1894	BG/7/GK/40 Aug 1904–Dec 1904	BG/7/GK/76 Dec 1912–Feb 1913
BG/7/GK/5 Oct 1894–Jan 1895	BG/7/GK/41 Dec 1904–Mar 1905	BG/7/GK/77 Feb 1913–April 1913
BG/7/GK/6 Feb 1895–May 1895	BG/7/GK/42 Mar 1905–Jun 1905	BG/7/GK/78 Apr 1913–Jun 1913
BG/7/GK/7 May 1895–Aug 1895	BG/7/GK/43 Jun 1905–Sep 1905	BG/7/GK/79 Jun 1913–Sep 1913
BG/7/GK/8 Aug 1895–Nov 1895	BG/7/GK/44 Sep 1905–Dec 1905	BG/7/GK/80 Sep 1913–Dec 1913
BG/7/GK/9 Feb 1896–May 1896	BG/7/GK/45 Dec 1905–Feb 1906	BG/7/GK/81 Dec 1913–Feb 1914
BG/7/GK/10 May 1896–Aug 1896	BG/7/GK/46 Feb 1906–May 1906	BG/7/GK/82 Feb 1914–Apr 1914
BG/7/GK/11 Aug 1896–Nov 1896	BG/7/GK/47 May 1906–Aug 1906	BG/7/GK/83 Apr 1914–Jul 1914
BG/7/GK/12 Dec 1896–Mar 1897	BG/7/GK/48 Aug 1906–Nov 1906	BG/7/GK/84 Jul 1914–Sep 1914
BG/7/GK/13 Mar 1897–Jun 1897	BG/7/GK/49 Nov 1906–Feb 1907	BG/7/GK/85 Sep 1914–Dec 1914
BG/7/GK/14 Jun 1897–Aug 1897	BG/7/GK/50 Feb 1907–May 1907	BG/7/GK/86 Dec 1914–Mar 1915
BG/7/GK/15 Aug 1897–Nov 1897	BG/7/GK/51 May 1907–Aug 1907	BG/7/GK/87 Mar 1915–Jun 1915
BG/7/GK/16 Feb 1898–Apr 1898	BG/7/GK/52 Aug 1907–Nov 1907	BG/7/GK/88 Jun 1915–Sep 1915
BG/7/GK/17 Apr 1898–Jul 1898	BG/7/GK/53 Nov 1907–Jan 1908	BG/7/GK/89 Sep 1915–Jan 1916
BG/7/GK/18 Jul 1898–Sep 1898	BG/7/GK/54 Feb 1908–Apr 1908	BG/7/GK/90 Jan 1916–May 1916
BG/7/GK/19 Sep 1898–Dec 1898	BG/7/GK/55 Apr 1908–Jul 1908	BG/7/GK/91 May 1916–Sep 1916
BG/7/GK/20 Mar 1898 – Dec 1898	BG/7/GK/56 Jul 1908–Sep 1908	BG/7/GK/92 Sep 1916–Jan 1917
BG/7/GK/21 Mar 1899–Jun 1899	BG/7/GK/57 Sep 1908–Dec 1908	BG/7/GK/93 Jan 1917–April 1917
BG/7/GK/22 Jun 1899–Sep 1899	BG/7/GK/58 Dec 1908–Feb 1909	BG/7/GK/94 Apr 1917–Aug 1917
BG/7/GK/23 Sep 1899–Nov 1899	BG/7/GK/59 Feb 1909–May 1909	BG/7/GK/95 Aug 1917–Jan 1918
BG/7/GK/24 Dec 1899–Mar 1900	BG/7/GK/60 May 1909–Jul 1909	BG/7/GK/96 Jan 1918–May 1918
BG/7/GK/25 Mar 1900–Jun 1900	BG/7/GK/61 Jul 1909–Oct 1909	BG/7/GK/97 May 1918–Oct 1918
BG/7/GK/26 Jun 1900–Sep 1900	BG/7/GK/62 Oct 1909–Jan 1910	BG/7/GK/98 Oct 1918–Jan 1919
BG/7/GK/27 Sep 1900–Dec 1900	BG/7/GK/63 Jan 1910–Mar 1910	BG/7/GK/99 Jan 1919–Jun 1919
BG/7/GK/28 Dec 1900–Mar 1901	BG/7/GK/64 Mar 1910–Jun 1910	BG/7/GK/100 Jun 1919–Oct 1919
BG/7/GK/29 Apr 1901–Jul 1901	BG/7/GK/65 Jun 1910–Sep 1910	BG/7/GK/101 Oct 1919–Jan 1920
BG/7/GK/30 Jul 1901–Nov 1901	BG/7/GK/66 Sep 1910–Dec 1910	BG/7/GK/102 Jan 1920–Mar 1920
BG/7/GK/31 Mar 1901 – Mar 1902	BG/7/GK/67 Dec 1910–Mar 1911	BG/7/GK/103 Mar 1920–Jun 1920
BG/7/GK/32 Mar 1902–Jul 1902	BG/7/GK/68 Mar 1911–May 1911	BG/7/GK/104 Jun 1920–Oct 1920
BG/7/GK/33 Jul 1902–Nov 1902	BG/7/GK/69 May 1911–Aug 1911	BG/7/GK/105 Oct 1920–Jan 1921
BG/7/GK/34 Nov 1902–Feb 1903	BG/7/GK/70 Aug 1911–Nov 1911	BG/7/GK/106 Jan 1921–May 1921
BG/7/GK/35 Mar 1903–Jun 1903	BG/7/GK/71 Nov 1911–Jan 1912	BG/7/GK/107 May 1921–Sep 1921
BG/7/GK/36 Jun 1903–Oct 1903	BG/7/GK/72 Feb 1912–Apr 1912	

The following example shows how information from the full registers can sometimes conflict with details from other sources:

Case study: Mary Jane Kane, born in about 1859, was the sister of my three times great-grandmother Christina Taylor (née Kane). She married a seaman called William Gibson in November 1875, only to pass away at the age of 30 at Belfast Workhouse on 27 February 1891, with the record noting that she was from 5 Cargill Street, and the cause of death as dementia.

As this was just before the available workhouse index records online, her case had to be searched for at PRONI, in volume BG/7/G/14, with her entry soon found on page 35, number 1389.

This record noted that she was aged 33, married, employed at the mill, Presbyterian, and that her 'disability' was a 'weak mind'. She was further noted as residing at 5 Cargill Street, and had been admitted to the workhouse on 7 February 1891. The record then notes that she either died or left the workhouse on 9 February 1891.

Note that additional records are also held at PRONI dealing with 'outdoor relief', for payments made to individuals who did not have to go into the workhouse.

Of equal interest may be the Medical Officer of Health reports for the City of Belfast, noting the state of health within the population. These can be found on the Wellcome Library catalogue at **https://search. wellcomelibrary.org** by typing in 'Medical Officer of Health Belfast', with various reports available from 1909 to 1972.

Don't forget also to try searches in the catalogue for an individual by their name only, as you just never know what might pop up.

Case study: The brother of my three times great-grandfather Cochrane Watton (p.153) was called William. I was surprised to discover a series of letters written by his wife Maggie to the prime minister of Northern Ireland, James Craig, seeking financial support due to her husband having been out of work for two years. The following is a typical extract from her letters, from correspondence dated 22 December 1922 (the spelling is as originally recorded):

> I take plivelage of writing to you as I am in very poor state owing to the want of work as my husband is out of work over 2 years and their is 6 children all young and I am just watting to get put out of my house owing to my rent been behind as I owe over 6 pounds in arearres in my book so I would be never so much thankful to you if you could help me in any way as the children is almost nacked for clothing and my beds is in a poor state. I even havent got a ticket for this relief coal. The only work my Husband got was a spell on the specials owing to him being ex service man. It is very hard to serve your king and country and not get a help from any one.
>
> (Source: Letters requesting financial assistance, Dec 1922–Feb 1926. PM/2/23/91, PRONI)

In a reply dated 19 January 1923, the Prime Minister's private secretary stated:

> The Prime Minister has asked me to forward you the enclosed donation and desires me to say that he trusts your husband will now remain in constant employment. He is very sorry to hear of your sad circumstances and would have sent a larger

amount but this is impossible owing to the many demands that are being made upon his purse at the present time.

Having received a helping hand, Maggie tried again over the next two years, receiving additional sums. The collection of correspondence includes all sorts of interesting gems, including notices to her husband to quit his property, and correspondence from the Belfast Council on Social Work confirming that 'all reports say they are very decent quiet people who have had a hard time owing to unemployment'. However, in early 1925 Maggie's luck finally ran out. In a letter dated 9 February from the secretary of the Belfast Council on Social Work to Colonel Spender at Stormont Castle, the following was noted:

We made a fresh enquiry on receipt of your letter and we are more satisfied than before that Mrs Watton is a begging letter writer and should not be encouraged as there is no distress in the case.

A letter was then sent to Maggie on 25 February, bluntly confirming that she would not be receiving any more payments from the Prime Minister, 'owing to the numerous calls that are being made upon his purse at the present time.'

TIP: Many Belfast folk who tried to claim poor relief whilst living in Britain were deported back to the city because they did not have the right of 'settlement'. You can find the names of some from the 1860s–1870s on Raymond's Co. Down website at **www.raymondscountydownwebsite.com**, or via the UK Parliamentary Papers site at **https://parlipapers.proquest.com** (accessible via subscribing institutions only).

Hospitals and asylums

The first mention of a hospital in Belfast dates from 1689, but it would not be until the late eighteenth century that more formalised efforts to produce hospital care for the population intensified.

From 1774, the Belfast Charitable Society provided medical relief at the Poor House at Clifton Street (p.35), annually offering hundreds of its citizens treatment. However, such relief was not extended to those who had lost their employment due to ill health, or to those who did not have the right of settlement. To address this deficiency, a General Dispensary was created in 1792, with funds raised by subscription, with its committee working in partnership with the Charitable Society.

In 1794, a Lying-In Hospital was created at a house in Donegall Street to assist destitute pregnant women, with Lady Harriet Skeffington as its first Patroness. In 1830, a purpose-built hospital facility was constructed within the grounds of the Charitable Society on the Antrim Road to continue its work, with newborn children given a supply of clothes upon their discharge from the premises. A year later, a Lying-In Dispensary was opened in William Street. The Lying-In Hospital moved to Townsend Street in 1904, and later became known as the Royal Belfast Maternity Hospital at a new site in 1933 on the Grosvenor Road, and from 2000, the Royal Jubilee Maternity Hospital.

In April 1797, a new Fever Hospital was opened in the town at Factory Row, in connection with the General Dispensary, initially with just six beds. The hospital, the first such institution to be created in Ireland, was soon superseded by the opening of the Belfast Hospital and Dispensary in October 1799. Patients admitted with fever would have their houses disinfected as a measure to try to contain any outbreak, and vaccination measures were taken to try to prevent smallpox outbreaks.

In the early to mid-nineteenth century, the poor state of the accommodation in a rapidly expanding town led to major health problems. In 1807, the Belfast Medical Society was established by the town's physicians and surgeons to try to make improvements with medical treatment. It barely lasted a year before its dissolution, but it was revived in 1822 following the opening in August 1817 of a new Belfast Hospital on Frederick Street (which later became the Belfast General Hospital in 1847, the Belfast Royal Hospital from 1875, and then the Royal Victoria Hospital from 1899). This not only catered for the treatment of the town's citizens but also aimed to provide medical training. A detailed history of the institution, and its predecessors, is available to read on the Wellcome Library at **https://wellcomecollection. org/works/dx74ku9k**. In 1903, the Royal Victoria Hospital moved to a new facility on the Falls Road, where it continues to this day. A register from the hospital from 1914 to 1916 is available on the PRONI website (see p.149). In 1920, Musgrave Park Hospital was also opened in the city.

With regards to the mental health of Belfast's inhabitants, a Lunatic Asylum was erected on the Grosvenor Road in May 1829, initially to hold 100 patients, but tripling that number within a few short years. Following its closure in 1913, the building was converted to be used by the Royal Belfast Maternity Hospital from 1933, whilst the asylum's work continued at the new Purdysburn Villa Colony, which became a hospital in 1948, and later Knockbracken Mental Health Services.

In the early 1830s, the town's hospitals had their work cut out for them, preparing for the arrival of influenza, and then a major wave of cholera from 1832. They were assisted by a Board of Health established in 1831, which constructed a temporary cholera hospital behind the Fever Hospital. With another wave of cholera in 1847, a new fever hospital was built on the site of the workhouse, relieving pressure on the general hospital. This facility was the forerunner of today's Belfast City Hospital.

In 1871, the Benn Ulster Eye, Ear and Throat Hospital was opened at Clifton Street, whilst a year later the Ulster Hospital for Women and Sick Children opened on Chichester Street, later moving to Mountpottinger in 1892. As the Ulster Hospital for Children and Women it was established on the Upper Newtownards Road in 1962, and since 2011 has been a teaching hospital for Queen's University.

In 1873, the Royal Belfast Hospital for Sick Children was opened on Queen Street, later moving to the Falls Road. In 1883, the Mater Infirmorum Hospital was established on the Crumlin Road in the city by the Sisters of Mercy. Despite being a Roman Catholic-run institution, it treated patients irrespective of their religious denomination, and later became a teaching hospital for Queen's University Belfast in 1903, with a maternity wing opening in 1945.

The Mater Infirmorum Hospital on the Crumlin Road today.

During the First World War, the Ulster Volunteer Force contributed thousands of recruits to the British Army. To assist with their care, a hospital was established at Craigavon House, known as the 'UVF Hospital', to deal with soldiers suffering from shell-shock, with a separate care facility established at Belfast Corporation's Exhibition Hall. The hospital continued its work after both world wars, but with the outbreak of the Troubles in 1969 it renamed itself as the Somme Hospital, to distinguish itself from the newly emerged paramilitary group that had styled itself as the UVF. A history of the facility can be found at **https://bit.ly/SommeHospital**.

In 1968, the Belfast Ophthalmic Hospital opened, later to be renamed Shaftesbury Square Hospital in 1969. It eventually closed in 2010.

Medical records can be a little difficult to source but can help to add extra detail to the brief recordings on death certificates, as well as from earlier periods in life. To locate surviving historical records, the Hospital Records Database from the National Archives in England can be consulted at **www.nationalarchives.gov.uk/hospitalrecords**. Many records are held at PRONI, as follows:

- Royal Victoria Hospital   HOS/2/1
- Belfast City Hospital   HOS/4/1
- Royal Maternity Hospital, Belfast   HOS/2/2; HOS/32/1
- Knockbracken Mental Health Services   HOS/28/1
- Royal Belfast Hospital for Sick Children   HOS/2/3
- Musgrave Park Hospital   HOS/4/2
- Ulster Hospital   HOS/22/1
- Ulster Hospital for Children and Women   HOS/22/2
- Belfast Ophthalmic Hospital   HOS/3/1
- Benn Hospital   HOS/3/2

As with workhouse records, the most recent records will be closed for privacy reasons.

Court records
When a wrong was committed in Belfast, it wasn't always enough to be able to just tell your ma about it! As with the rest of the UK and Ireland, not all of Belfast's citizens abided by the rule of law, with many being hauled up before the courts.

One of the greatest tragedies of the Four Courts fire in 1922 in Dublin was that a great many of the historical records concerning the assize courts for serious crimes were destroyed. Whilst some do survive, there is better coverage for the petty sessions' records from the mid-nineteenth century, although PRONI does not have a guide to these on its website. Law and order were policed on the streets by special constables in the early nineteenth century, from 1836 by the Royal Irish Constabulary, and from 1922 the Royal Ulster Constabulary (p.146)

Belfast's surviving petty sessions records from 1853 to 1991 are catalogued as a series under HA/1/14. In most cases, you will likely find a write-up of the cases featured at the local sessions' hearings through the contemporary newspapers.

Case study: My five times great-grandfather Arthur Taylor was hauled before the Belfast Police Court on two occasions in 1868 and 1869, at the approximate age of 71.

The first report from the *Belfast Morning News* on 12 June 1868 flags up his initial misdemeanour:

BELFAST POLICE COURT
Arthur Taylor was charged by Sub-Constable Pickett with being drunk yesterday in charge of a horse and car in Great Patrick Street. Car Inspector Duff states that this was the first charge against the prisoner. In reply to Mr. Orme, Taylor stated that he had been driving a car for 40 years. Fined 5s and costs.

Clearly Arthur was having issues controlling his vehicle, as again noted in the *Belfast Newsletter* of 18 March 1869:

BELFAST POLICE COURT, Yesterday, the presiding magistrates at this court were J. C. O'Donnell, Esq., R.M., and E. Orme, Esq, R.M...
   Arthur Taylor, car-driver, Curtis Street, was summoned, at the instance of the Mayor, Aldermen and Burgesses, for driving his cab on the wrong side of the street, on the 10th inst., whereby a gentleman's carriage was injured. The defendant made a satisfactory apology for his misconduct, and the charge was withdrawn.

For the assize records, PRONI holds some records of the Clerks of Crown and Peace, who administered the county courts. Crown Books of the Quarter Session from 1890 onwards are catalogued under ANT/1/1/A/7 (continuing to /20), whilst Belfast County Court Sittings Crown and

Appeal Books 1963–1973 are found under ANT/1/1/A/22 (continuing to /25). Indictments and Pleas at Belfast are found from 1900 onwards under BELF/1/1/1/1 (continuing to /92 for records up to 1973). Prisoner files at Belfast Prison are included under HA/9/2, covering the period from 1887 to 1973, many of them for political offences, although only details on appeals and releases are included from 1950 onwards. However, many recent records may be closed for privacy purposes.

The ruins of Crumlin Road Courthouse. The building first opened in 1850, and has seen several large fires since its closure in 1998.

It is always worth doing a keyword search for an ancestor in the PRONI catalogue. A search for a relative called William Watton brings up an interesting description of a case brought against him and several others in 1912, catalogued under BELF/1/2/2/22/169. The case is described as 'The King v John Walker, James McCullough, George Bradshaw and William Watton re: accusations of slander against the citizens of Belfast', but unfortunately, despite its age, the record is still noted as closed to access. However, the information given is enough to facilitate a search of the British Newspaper Archive (p.48), which reveals a story from the *Freeman's Journal* on 14 August 1912, in which the four men listed are noted as having provoked a sectarian riot at the shipyard, in a period of tensions over Home Rule, just a month before the signing of the Ulster Covenant (p.11).

The recent Troubles are well documented in the press. PRONI also has a *Conflict related court records* guide available at **www.nidirect.gov. uk/articles/conflict-related-court-records**, and a separate guide to *Conflict related inquest records* at **www.nidirect.gov.uk/articles/conflict-**

related-inquest-records. The Prisons Memory Archive of 161 recorded interviews carried out from 2006–2007 with individuals connected to Armagh Gaol, the Maze and Long Kesh can be consulted also via **www. prisonsmemoryarchive.com**.

One other record set to be aware of is that of the grand juries. PRONI's *Your Family Tree 19: Grand Jury Records* guide includes a brief discussion of the availability of records for Belfast, most of which are included in the County Antrim section, with some additional holdings for the city from 1940 to 1969.

Sport

Historically, there have been many sports where Belfast folk have competed and sought to unwind from their weekly work efforts, including football (soccer), Gaelic football and hurling, rugby, cricket and hockey.

One of the greatest resources for tracing sports history in Belfast is the city's long published *Ireland's Saturday Night* newspaper (delivered weekly by yours truly in Carrickfergus for several years as a child!), with editions from 1894 to 2008 available on the British Newspaper Archive (p.48). From 1874 to 1895, the title was previously known as *Ulster Saturday Night*.

> **TIP:** PRONI has an *Alphabetical index to Sports Records* at **www. nidirect.gov.uk/publications/sporting-associations-index**, detailing many records from clubs and sports in Belfast and beyond.

Football

Several of today's major football teams in Belfast were created in the late nineteenth century. The oldest of Belfast's clubs, and indeed, the oldest Irish club, is Cliftonville FC, founded by John McCredy McAlery in 1879. Its history can be read at **https://cliftonvillefc.net/club-history-chapter-1/** and **https://en.wikipedia.org/wiki/Cliftonville_F.C.**

Established in 1882, Glentoran FC's history can be read at **https://en.wikipedia.org/wiki/Glentoran_F.C.** and the 'History' section of the club website at **www.glentoran.com**. Its main rival, Linfield FC, was founded just four years later in 1886, initially as an athletics club, by workers at the Ulster Spinning Company's Linfield Mill. Linfield's story is explored on its club website at **www.linfieldfc.com/history.aspx** and at **https://en.wikipedia.org/wiki/Linfield_F.C.** A club gallery with some historical team photos is available at **http://gallery.linfieldfc.com**, whilst records from the club from 1916 to 1917 are available at PRONI under T3824, and from 1934 to 1972 under D3852.

Belfast Celtic FC was a team formed in 1891, which played at Celtic Park in the city until 1949, after which it withdrew from the Irish League for political reasons. Prior to this it had been Linfield's greatest rival. Its history is wonderfully explored by the Belfast Celtic Society at **www.belfastceltic.org**, which also runs a museum at the Park Shopping Centre on the Donegall Road, built on the team's former ground.

For the story of the Crusaders FC in north Belfast, established in 1898, visit **https://crusadersfootballclub.com/history and https://en.wikipedia.org/wiki/Crusaders_F.C.**

The home to international football in Northern Ireland is at Windsor Park in Belfast, with its history explored at **https://en.wikipedia.org/wiki/Windsor_Park**. For a history of the Irish Football Association, founded in Belfast in 1880, visit **www.irishfa.com/irish-football-association/about-the-ifa**. A list of former (and current) international players for Northern Ireland can be found at **https://en.wikipedia.org/wiki/List_of_Northern_Ireland_international_footballers**.

Irish Football Association papers from 1880 to 1985 are at PRONI under D4196, but access is restricted.

Gaelic football and hurling

Casement Park (*Páirc Mhic Ásmaint*), on the Andersonstown Road in West Belfast, has been the main stadium for Gaelic football in Belfast since 1953, the ground being home to the Antrim side, and also to the Ulster Hurling Championship. A short history is available at **www.casementpark.ie/about-casement/**.

The Belfast Gaels or 'Pioneers' were the first Gaelic Athletics Club founded in Belfast, in 1885, followed soon by hurling clubs such as the Belfast Harps and Divis Rangers. The Antrim GAA site hosts a brief history at **https://antrim.gaa.ie/our-county/history**.

The Wolfe Tones GAC was founded at Greencastle in 1935, with its history available to read at **http://wolfetonesgaa.ie/history-stair/**. It continued until the 1970s, when its ground closed to facilitate the M2 construction, but was resurrected in 2019.

In South Belfast, St Malachy's is the oldest GAA club, established in 1936, and still plays today (**https://antrim.gaa.ie/clubs/st-malachys**). St Colmcille's GAA club briefly existed at Ballyhackamore on the Upper Newtownards Road in East Belfast, from the 1950s until the early 1970s. Its successor in the area today is the cross-community East Belfast GAA, founded in 2020.

Rugby

The earliest rugby teams in Belfast were founded in the nineteenth century, including teams such as Northern Ireland FC and Queen's

University. The games were initially regulated by the Northern Football Union of Ireland, before its merger with the Irish Football Union in 1879. The records of the Irish Rugby Football Union's Ulster Branch, based in Belfast, are available from 1886 to 1983 at PRONI under D3867.

The home of Ulster Rugby is Ravenhill Stadium (aka Kingspan Stadium) on Belfast's Ravenhill Park, with the first game played there on 12 January 1924. A history is available at **https://en.wikipedia.org/ wiki/Ravenhill_Stadium**.

The stadium hosts the Ulster Schools' Cup, which has existed since 1876, and which has been won by Methody (p.121) the most times, as well as the Ulster Towns' Cup, created in 1883.

Cricket

The North of Ireland Cricket Club was founded in the city in 1859, and now forms part of the Belfast Harlequins at Derrymore. Its history is explored at **https://en.wikipedia.org/wiki/North_of_Ireland_Cricket_ Club** and **www.cricketeurope.com/DATABASE/ARTICLESHISTORY/ articles/000005/000505.shtml**, whilst its ledger from 1892 to 1918 is at PRONI under D4189/F/1, with additional papers under D4286.

Cliftonville Cricket Club was founded in 1870 at Enfield, later merging with Greenisland in 1979 and then Academy Cricket Club in 2017 to form Cliftonville Academy Cricket Club. Its history is at **www. cliftonvilleacademy.com/cliftonville-cc-history/**.

Affiliated to Methody College, the Cooke Collegians Cricket Club existed from 1880 to 1999, with its story explored at **www.collegiansclub. org/index_option_com_content_view_article_id_220_Itemid_290.html**.

Cregagh Cricket Club has been based at Cregagh Memorial Grounds at Gibson Park Avenue since 1906, joining the Northern Cricket Union in 1920. The club's history can be read at **www.cregaghcricketclub.co.uk/ history**, which includes a Roll of Honour from the First World War.

The records of the Belfast Cricket League 1902–1977 are at PRONI under D3298, whilst records for St Mary's Cricket Club 1927–1970 are under D4248.

TIP: Several of the older schools in Belfast have alumni associations with a variety of sports teams, such as the Royal Belfast Academic Institution's Instonians at **www.instonians.org** and the Methody-affiliated Cooke Collegians, with its history at **www.collegiansclub.org**.

Hockey

The Ulster branch of the Irish Hockey Association was founded in 1896. The Ulster Hockey site at **https://ulsterhockey.com/125-archives/** hosts histories of several clubs from Belfast, including the Victorians ladies' team, established by former pupils from Victoria College Belfast in 1935, and Cliftonville's men's team, founded in 1896.

Papers from the Ulster Women's Hockey Union 1905–1993 are at PRONI under D3982, whilst records from Osborne Hockey Club 1909–1914 are found under D3888.

Theatres

For a history of several of Belfast's finest theatres, including the Lyric, the Ulster Hall, and the Grand Opera House, as well as the former Royal Hippodrome Theatre, visit the 'Music Hall and Theatre History Site Dedicated to Arthur Lloyd 1839–1904', at **www.arthurlloyd.co.uk/ BelfastTheatres.htm**.

A timeline for the history of theatre in Northern Ireland is available online from the Linen Hall Library at **www.digitaltheatrearchive. com/timelines**. It details the changing fortunes of theatres, from the first recorded performance in Belfast in 1736, the decline of popularity of theatre-going following the United Irishmen uprising in 1798 and throughout much of the nineteenth century, and the renewal of interest throughout the twentieth century.

The library's Theatre and Performing Arts collection can be explored at **www.linenhall.com/collections/theatre-and-performing-arts/**.

The Grand Opera House on Great Victoria Street first opened its doors in 1895.

Chapter 8

OCCUPATIONS

Following Belfast's grant of a charter in 1613 to form a corporation, it has evolved from a market trading charter town in the north of Ireland into an industrial powerhouse and capital city of Northern Ireland. Over the last four centuries, its inhabitants have worked in a variety of roles to earn a crust and feed their families, from merchants and manufacturers, to shipbuilders and linen producers. Many of the city's population worked within Belfast directly, whilst others played their part in services beyond its boundaries, and even beyond the island of Ireland.

In this chapter, I will examine some of the resources that can help to tell their stories, and where to find them.

Businesses

The records of businesses can provide an extraordinary insight into their development if they have survived, although they may not always be of immense use from a genealogical research point of view. If an ancestor was a merchant with a small operation, the records may certainly provide a wonderful insight into challenges faced on a daily basis, but with larger companies you may find it difficult to locate specific references to employees, particularly if hired as day labourers before the twentieth century.

Surviving records may exist in a number of forms, from letter books of correspondence (both drawn up and received), minute books, wage books, cash books and accounts, patents, legal papers, and a great deal more. Some of these might still be retained by the firms in question, whilst others may be held at PRONI. The archive's *Business records* guide can be consulted at **www.nidirect.gov.uk/publications/business-records**.

The *Belfast Gazette* newspaper (p.165) is a useful resource for business research, as it carries announcements of appointments and retirements within companies, the closures of companies, and in some cases even bankruptcy proceedings. Street directories (p.103) can also be a great resource to help trace a company's history, not just by looking for the names of employees and the companies' registered addresses but also by looking for trade advertisements, which in some cases may even show drawn images of the buildings within which they were housed, or the products that they sold. Newspapers (p.162) provide yet another very useful resource for tracing company activities across time.

For earlier times in the city, *The Town Book of the Corporation of Belfast 1613–1816*, compiled in 1892 by Robert M. Young, from the original town book manuscripts, and reprinted in 2008, names many of the merchants and craftsmen who worked, lived and traded in the city within this period.

The linen trade
As noted in Chapter 1, the linen trade dominated the lives of many folk in Belfast, particularly women, who worked in a variety of roles in the mills from doffers and scutchers, to spinners and weavers, as well as those who managed the staff and sold the wares produced.

In addition to the regular street directories listing workers and firms in the city, a comprehensive history of the linen industry in Belfast and across Ulster can be found in *The Irish Linen Trade Hand-Book and Directory* from 1876, as presented to the Belfast Chamber of Commerce, a useful resource available through the Internet Archive at **https://archive.org/details/irishlinentrade00smitgoog**. On Google Books (**https://books.google.com**) you can also find an earlier directory, *The Power Mills Directory of Great Britain and Ireland*, from 1866.

PRONI holds all sorts of records of interest concerning the industry. In addition to the various mills and factories, for example, are treasures such as fifty release certificates for workers from 1861 to 1914 employed at various mills, including Ligoniel Spinning Company, Crumlin Road Mills, Brookfield Mills, Suffolk Linen Company, Wolfhill Mill, Ballysillan Spinning Company, and the York Street Flax Spinning Company Ltd, catalogued under D2966/102/2.

PRONI also has various trade union records for textiles workers:

- The Flax and other Textile Workers Trade Union, 1890–1959 (COM/76/13)
- The Flax and other Textile Workers Trade Union, 1894–1958 (D1050/7)

- The Irish Linen Lappers and Warehouse Workers Trade Union, 1893–1926 (COM/76/14)
- The Loom Overlookers Trade Union, 1875–1963 (COM/76/16-17)
- The Northern Ireland Textile Workers Trade Union, 1907–1964 (COM/76/21)
- Tailors and Garment Workers Trade Union, 1927–1932 (COM/76/32A-32B)
- The Beetling Engineers Trade Union, 1912–1921 (COM/76/3)

Newspapers (p.162) can be a useful resource for tales of mill workers.

Case study: My three times great-grandfather Thomas Graham worked as a reeling master in the mills for most of his life. A story concerning him in the *Banner of Ulster* on Tuesday, 10 December 1850 noted him being hauled up at the Belfast Police Court (p.1–2). As the reeling master at the Hull, Harden & Co. mill, he was prosecuted for the assault of a millworker, and fined 2s 6d as a consequence.

The charge was that a millworker, Rebecca Curliss, was twelve minutes late for her shift on the previous Wednesday. Upon arrival she found another girl in her place, and was approached by Thomas who apparently scolded her for being late. She replied that work was available easily enough elsewhere, at which point he told her 'not to be impertinent'. When she refused to leave, he was said to have threatened to 'knock her down stairs' and pushed her, at which point she hit him and gave him a black eye. At this point he was alleged to have dragged her away to the bottom of the works, before she was subsequently dismissed by the works' manager. Speaking in Thomas's defence, Mr Hull, one of the mill owners, was reported as making the following claim about him:

After some conversation as to whether Mr Hull should be examined, that gentleman was sworn, and stated that he considered the character and conduct of the defendant, who had been a long time in his employment, to be very correct, and anything but that of a harsh over-looker. The complainant was paid off by himself on Saturday, and she made not the slightest reference to the occurrence about which she had just given evidence.

After sentencing, a Mr O'Rorke from the mill claimed that three witnesses were prepared to step forward to give a very different account to that by the complainant, but the magistrate refused to re-open the case.

Thomas was again in trouble in 1872 for a breach of the Factory Act, whilst working as an overlooker at the York Street Flax Spinning Company Ltd on Henry Street, one of the largest flax spinning mills in the world. He was prosecuted at Belfast Petty Sessions Court for employing six females in the reeling room after 6 p.m. on 12 November, a breach of the Act. In this case, the source was an HM Factories Inspectorate report for the half year ending April 1873, located via the UK Parliamentary Papers platform (p.130), which detailed his case. It stated that:

> The Defendants having proved that the offences were committed by the overlooker (Thos. Graham) in contravention of their positive orders, and without their knowledge, consent, or connivance, and having summoned Graham into Court to answer the charge, the offences were transferred to him.

It seems that Thomas was only formally prosecuted for employing two of the six women late, and was fined £2 penalty and 6s 6d in costs. His defence was noted as follows:

> The Defendant who has held his present position as overlooker for 20 years without previous offence, acknowledged that he was in fault, and urged extenuating circumstances.

The magistrate was lenient. For the charges concerning the other four women he stated that they were:

> Withdrawn on payment of costs, as I considered a fine of £2 14s 6d sufficient punishment for a working man.
> (Source: Reports of Inspectors of Factories to Secretary of State for Home Dept., November 1872–April 1873, p.59, UK Parliamentary Papers, accessed via **https://archives. parliament.uk/online-resources/parliamentary-papers**)

Shipbuilding

PRONI contains many records for shipping firms, such as the Head Line Shipping Company from 1897 to 1970, catalogued under D3117, Workman Clark and Company (HAR/1/K), and, of course, for Harland and Wolff, catalogued under a variety of accession numbers, most notably under D2805. A search on the PRONI catalogue under this accession number provides a detailed history of the records collected by PRONI and how they were catalogued.

Amongst the potentially useful Harland and Wolff records are wage books from 1861 to 1952, which could well be useful for family history research. However, only a small part of the Harland and Wolff archive is open to the public, with the company's stated approach being that 'We regard all manner of personnel records and related material as strictly confidential and it is our strict company policy to refuse access for general research purposes.' Nevertheless, it is possible to ask PRONI to consider a request, from which they can advise if suitable records are held, and if needs be, they can contact Harland and Wolff to seek permission for the records to be made available for consultation.

The PRONI *Maritime Records* guide, found within its Local History Series of leaflets, lists the archive collection numbers for many of the most famous maritime businesses in Belfast, including Harland and

Belfast's most iconic landmarks, the twin gantry cranes of Samson and Goliath at the Harland and Wolff yard, commenced work in 1969 and 1974.

Wolff, the North of Ireland Shipbuilding Company, the Belfast Steamship Company, and the Belfast Ropeworks, whilst its Education Leaflets include one on RMS *Titanic*. A list of shipowners in Belfast from 1860 can be found on Ulster Ancestry (**www.ulsterancestry.com**).

Although it may be difficult to research shipworkers from the accessible company records, there are other sources that can help with research, beyond the basic records of births, marriages, deaths, and censuses. For example, for an accidental death in the yard, it may be possible to apply to see the records of a coroner's inquest, which are again held by PRONI.

If your ancestor was skilled worker in the yards, it is likely that he would have been a member of a trade union. Findmypast's 'Britain, Trade Union Membership Registers' collection includes records of the *United Society of Boilermakers and Iron Shipbuilders 1871–1947*. A search for my great-grandfather's brother, a boilermaker called Edwin (son of Edwin on p.12), shows that he joined the Belfast 3 branch of the union on 20 March 1912, aged 28, and again on 21 April 1927, aged 43.

For those involved in carpentry, the database also includes entries for the *General Union of Carpenters & Joiners (1886–1920)*, the *Amalgamated Society of Carpenters & Joiners (1886–1920)*, the *Amalgamated Society of Carpenters, Cabinetmakers & Joiners (1918–1921)*, and the *Amalgamated Society of Woodworkers (1921–1931)*. In some cases, entries in the registers may name dependants, the date of superannuation payments commencing, and even death.

Trade unions

In addition to the records for boilermakers and carpenters and joiners, Findmypast's 'Britain, Trade Union Membership Registers' collection also includes records for the following unions with Belfast branches:

- Amalgamated Society of Lithographic Artists, Designers, Engravers & Process Workers, 1885–1919
- Amalgamated Society of Lithographic Printers, 1880–1932
- Amalgamated Society of Railway Servants, 1872–1913
- Amalgamated Society of Paper Makers, 1914–1918
- Incorporated Association Of Assistant Masters In Secondary School, 1919
- Operative Bricklayers' Society, 1914–1916
- National Union Of Railwaymen, 1913–1928
- National Union Of Printing & Paper Workers, 1914–1919
- Typographical Association, 1915–1919
- Workers' Union, 1913–1920

Many detail membership of their unions, whilst some include records of those who were killed during service in the First World War.

In addition to trade union records for textiles workers (p.141), PRONI also holds some further collections, such as the following:

- Northern Ireland Post Office Clerks' Association, 1881–1953 (D1050/1)
- National Federation of Building Trade Operatives, 1956–1963 (D1050/2)
- National Amalgamated Union of Life Assurance Workers, 1930–1956 (D1050/3)
- Northern Ireland Butchers' Association, 1925–1950 (D1050/4)
- United Operative Plumbers' and Domestic Engineers' Association, 1867–1940 (D1050/5)
- Belfast and District Trade Union Council, 1899–1983 (D1050/6)
- Belfast Printing Trades Employers' Association, 1896–1981 (D3759)
- The Belfast and Dublin Locomotive Engine Drivers and Firemen's Trade Union, 1895–1940 (COM/76/4)
- The Belfast Coopers Trade Union, 1891–1962 (COM/76/6)
- The Belfast Hairdressers Trade Union,1892–1928 (COM/76/7)
- The Belfast Operative House and Ship Painters and Decorators Trade Union, 1877–1930 (COM/76/8)
- The Belfast Operative House and Ship Plasterers, 1880–1934 (COM/76/9)
- The Belfast Packing Case Makers Trade Union, 1890–1928 (COM/76/10)
- The North of Ireland Butchers Trade Union, 1937–1940 (COM/76/24)
- Belfast Operative House Painters' Trade Union, 1877–1937 (D1050/10)

Law and order

A useful overview of various historical Irish police forces is available at **www.royalirishconstabulary.com**, which includes information on the Royal Irish Constabulary (RIC) and its northern successor from June 1922, the Royal Ulster Constabulary (RUC).

An 'Index to the Report of Belfast Special Constables', 1812–1816, held at PRONI under D46/1, is available on Ulster Ancestry in its County Antrim section, listing constables appointed, and the pages where they are referenced.

RIC service records are held at TNA, but have been digitised and made available on Findmypast. Collections available include 'Ireland, Royal Irish Constabulary Service Records 1816–1922', 'Ireland, Royal Irish Constabulary Pensions 1826–1925', and 'Ireland, Royal Irish Constabulary History & Directories'. The latter includes six different publications printed between 1871 and 1920, and sixty-eight pieces from the archive's HO 184 collection.

RIC officers acted as enumerators during the censuses, handing out household schedules and collecting them after census night. For the 1901 and 1911 censuses, you may therefore come across the names of police ancestors on the Form N or Form B part of the schedules (p.93). Police barracks enumerated in the census were done so on a Form H, rather than a Form A, but an unfortunate problem with some of these returns is that many officers were recorded by their initials only.

Another resource that can help you to locate Belfast-based officers in the 1911 census is Keith Winters' site at **https://winters-online.net/RIC-Barracks/**. As well as census transcripts, this identifies many barracks' locations in the city, with some additional resources such as newspaper obituaries of officers.

The Police Service of Northern Ireland (PSNI) website at **www.psni.police.uk** includes an 'Our History' section within its 'About Us' section. This has a Police Museum, and a 'Genealogy' page, with details on searches that it can provide into RIC service records from 1822 to 1922, as well as from various printed RIC lists held at the museum. For service within the later RUC, the current PSNI museum has a series of service record cards that continue up to 1977, after which they have been computerised. A similar set-up exists for records of the PSNI itself, which replaced the RUC in 2001. There is a 75-year closure period for access to these cards by the general public, although ex-policemen or their family members can view more recent records if the relevant proof of relationship to the officer concerned is supplied.

The Police Roll of Honour Trust website at **www.policememorial.org.uk/** carries memorials to members of both the RUC and the modern PSNI. For police ancestors decorated during military or police service, the Medal Society of Ireland website at **www.msoi.eu** is worth consulting.

The British military

Many citizens from Belfast have served with the British armed forces, even before Ireland joined the United Kingdom in 1801. Historical records of the UK's armed forces are held centrally at the National Archives in London, which hosts several useful online guides to help at **www.nationalarchives.gov.uk/help-with-your-research**. More recent service records are held by the UK Ministry of Defence **www.gov.uk/get-copy-military-service-records**.

The British Army

The Barracks on the Lower Falls traces its history from the seventeenth century to the Blitz of 1941, with all that remains today being the old army gym that now forms North Queen Street Community Centre. A detailed account of the site can be read at **www.belfasthistoryproject. com/thebarrack**.

For soldiers from Belfast serving in the British Army prior to the First World War, the most useful records are those evidencing their discharge to pension or of service with a militia. Prior to Partition, soldiers could be discharged at either Royal Hospital Kilmainham in Dublin, or at the Royal Hospital Chelsea in London, with most being out-pensioners. A pension was payable to soldiers who had served for more than twelve years in the army, and as such the records will not contain information on those who left early, who were killed in action or who died early in service.

Chelsea pension records have been made available at Findmypast UK as the 'British Army Service Records' collection. They provide brief service details, useful biographical details such as place of attestation and birth, physical descriptions, and more. The collection also includes militia records from 1806 to 1915. As with the Chelsea pension records, the militia records offer details on military service, but also on previous employment.

For soldiers discharged at Kilmainham, Findmypast has the 'British Army Pensioners, Royal Hospital Kilmainham, Ireland, 1783–1822' collection. The site also hosts other datasets, such as its 'Irish Regimental Enlistment Registers 1877–1924', Army Lists, muster rolls, officer promotions, and widows' pension forms.

Ancestry also hosts various British military records, including its 'UK, Royal Hospital, Chelsea: Regimental Registers of Pensioners, 1713–1882' collection, medal rolls, army lists, and its 'UK, British Army Muster Books and Pay Lists, 1812–1817' collection. Regimental description books are also found in the 'UK, Regimental Registers of Service, 1756–1900', which may provide background information, including a physical description, place of origin and previous employment, which can be very useful if a soldier did not survive or serve long enough to receive a pension.

Belfast folk were heavily involved during the First World War. At a time of great tension over the issue of Home Rule, many volunteered from the ranks of the unionist-led Ulster Volunteer Force, determined to do service for the Crown and to be rewarded with the abolition of the devolution issue once and for all as a reward. Whilst Belfast's Protestant soldiers served in many regiments, the 36th Ulster Division was home to most, which fought at many theatres, including the Somme, paying a heavy toll. Conversely, many members of the nationalist Irish Volunteers also signed up for the opposite reason – to make sure that their loyalty was rewarded with the implementation of Home Rule, granted and then suspended in 1914, as the war broke out. They too served with distinction in the 10th and 16th (Irish) divisions of the British Army.

PRONI carries an outstanding guide to its First World War resources at **www.nidirect.gov.uk/sites/default/files/2021-11/first-world-war-sources. pdf**. This not only documents military resources held at the archive but also much on civilian life, including resource pertaining to the 'Decade of Centenaries' from 1912 to 1923, covering topics from Home Rule and the republican campaign, to church war memorials and contemporary diaries.

A useful overview of the key efforts of the war can be found via The Long, Long Trail, at **www.longlongtrail.co.uk**. MilitaryArchives.ie (p.156) has also put together a guide detailing the known Irish regiments in existence up to 31 July 1922, accessible at **https://bit.ly/BritishArmy-IrishRegiments**.

About 40 per cent of British Army service records from the period have survived, catalogued by the UK National Archives under WO 363 and WO 364. Ancestry has digitised these within two separate collections, 'British Army WWI Service Records, 1914–1920' and 'British Army WWI Pension Records, 1914–1920', whilst Findmypast lists them within its 'British Army Service Records' collection. FamilySearch also holds the records in its 'United Kingdom, World War I Service Records, 1914–1920' set, although these can only be accessed within a LDS family history centre (p.33).

Many additional datasets from the war are on the main vendor sites. For example, Findmypast, Ancestry and MyHeritage have databases listing those injured who were entitled to the Silver War Badge from 1914 to 1920, whilst Findmypast and Ancestry host records of the Committee of the Irish National War Memorial's eight volume 'Ireland's Memorial Record 1914–1918', listing many of those who died. Ancestry, Findmypast and The Genealogist also have 'De Ruvigny's Roll of Honour', listing officer deaths from all armed forces, and the 'UK, Soldiers Died in the Great War, 1914–1919' collection, as produced by Her Majesty's Stationery Office (HMSO) in 1921.

PRONI hosts a digitised register of war casualties who were treated in the Royal Victoria Hospital, Belfast, between September 1914 and November 1916, alongside a corresponding names index. To access this, visit the site's Decade of Centenaries section at **www.nidirect.gov.**

uk/articles/decade-centenaries and select from the right-hand menu. Further afield, TheGenealogist (www.thegenealogist.gov.uk) holds daily and weekly casualty lists from 1914 to 1920, as sourced from War Office Casualty Lists. Forces War Records (www.forces-war-records. co.uk) also provides access to these records, alongside other collections for all the British armed forces.

For Belfast folk who may have become prisoners of war, visit the International Red Cross site at https://grandeguerre.icrc.org for free-to-access digitised prisoners lists. Volunteers from the city also served with the British Red Cross – they can be searched for via www.redcross.org. uk/about-us/our-history.

The Commonwealth War Graves Commission at www.cwgc.org lists the names of Irish men and women who gave their lives in the conflict, including free-to-access documentation on the arrangements for their burials, whilst the Irish War Memorials site at www.irishwarmemorials. ie may also help. Eddie Connolly hosts the *Presbyterian Church in Ireland Roll of Honour* for both world wars at www.eddiesextracts.com. Around 300 bank officials of the Belfast Banking Company Limited, Northern Banking Company Limited and Northern Bank Ltd, who died in the two world wars and the Troubles are commemorated in a memorial and roll of honour at https://northernbankwarmemorials.blogspot.com.

The NAI has placed soldiers' wills online for free consultation at www. genealogy.nationalarchives.ie. For the wills of Belfast-born soldiers who served in other British regiments consult Find a Will (https://probatesearch. service.gov.uk) and ScotlandsPeople (www.scotlandspeople.gov.uk).

The Commonwealth War Graves Commission website.

An ongoing project to document Irish survivors from service in the First World War is available at **www.worldwar1veterans.com**.

The Western Front Association also offers resources at **www. westernfrontassociation.com**, including a useful explanation about some 6 million First World War pension record cards rescued from destruction by the organisation, which can be read at **www.westernfrontassociation. com/ancestry-pension-records**. These are now available through Ancestry's sister site, Fold3 (**www.fold3.com**), as the 'UK, WW1 Pension Ledgers and Index Cards, 1914–1923' collection. Talks from the Western Front Association given in Belfast at PRONI can be found on the archive's YouTube channel at **www.youtube.com/@PRONIonline**.

Belfast was hit by the Luftwaffe in devastating Blitz attacks on the nights of 7 April, 15 April (Easter Tuesday) and 4 May 1941. Incendiary bombs were used to devastate parts of the city, including the centre and docks areas, with an unprepared Belfast having never really believed that it would be a target, being located just at the edge of the range of the German planes. In a rare showing of solidarity, the neutral Irish Free State sent several firemen and tenders over the border to help extinguish the flames, with the Taoiseach Eamonn de Valera stating that of the Belfast population that 'their sorrows in the present instance are also our sorrows; and I want to say to them that any help we can give to them in the present time we will give to them whole-heartedly, believing that were the circumstances reversed they would also give us their help whole-heartedly.'

It is a period that was remembered all too well by my uncle Robert Paton (1939–2022), who as a very young child recalled his family leaving their house at Whitewell Crescent in the middle of the night to find shelter during one of the raids; along the way he was accidentally dropped by my grandfather, and suffered a bang on the head as a consequence (hence his acute memory of the night!). During the raids, the locals sought shelter in the nearby hills and hedges in a practice known as 'ditching'. Many houses were damaged during the raids, including my grandparents' home, prompting them to relocate to the house next door shortly after.

More than 1,050 people died as a result of these raids, with much infrastructure destroyed, including eighteen schools and eleven churches. For Belfast's experience of the Second World War, visit **www. ww2ni.com**, whilst PRONI's Flickr account hosts graphically animated images of Belfast from the Blitz.

TIP: A list of casualties from the Belfast Blitz attacks can be found at **www.niwarmemorial.org/collections/blitz-victims**, in PRONI catalogued under LA/65/3/AG/2, and in Brian Barton's book *The Belfast Blitz: The City in the War Years* (2015). A list of those who lost their lives working for the Belfast Civil Defence Service can be found on Eddie's Extracts (p.49).

The Northern Ireland War Memorial Museum (p.41) on Talbot Street includes a presentation on the Blitz, as well as other displays, such as on the presence of American GIs and the role of the Ulster Home Guard. The Royal Ulster Rifles Regimental Museum (p.42) on Bedford Street includes displays on the regiment's involvement in India and France during the Second World War.

Following the outbreak of the Troubles in 1969, the Ulster Defence Regiment was established in Northern Ireland, replacing the Ulster Special Constabulary or 'B-Specials'. It soon became the largest regiment of the British Army and existed until 1992, at which point it merged with the Royal Irish Rangers. Wikipedia has a detailed article on the regiment at **http://en.wikipedia.org/wiki/Ulster_Defence_Regiment**.

The UDR's Regimental Association can be visited at **www.ulsterdefenceregimentassociation.com**, with the site including a roll of honour.

The Royal Navy
If your ancestor was in the UK's senior service, the UK National Archives' Research Guides website at **www.nationalarchives.gov.uk/help-with-your-research/research-guides** offers many guides on Royal Navy- related topics, along with searchable databases, such as Royal Navy Ratings 1853–1923, Royal Naval Officers' Service Records 1756–1931, Wills of Royal Navy and Royal Marines personnel 1786–1882, Women's Royal Naval Service Records 1917–1919, and Royal Naval Division Service Records 1914–1919, detailing the reservist seamen who fought alongside the army in the trenches during the war. Guides which include searchable holdings have a white tick in a green circle listed beside them. There is also a useful guide for researching ex-sailors who became Greenwich Pensioners at **www.nationalarchives.gov.uk/records/research-guides/royal-navy-rating-pension.htm**.

A database of First World War Royal Naval Division casualties is also available on both Findmypast and Ancestry. Findmypast hosts further collections for 'British Royal Navy & Royal Marines Service and Pension

Case study: Not all naval service records from the First World War *are* online. Take for example the service of my three times great-grandfather Cochrane McLaughlin Watton, a painter and decorator from 35 Barrow Street in Belfast. I was stunned to discover from an online medal roll that a 'Cochrane Watton' had apparently signed up to the Royal Marines Labour Corps and been awarded the Victory and British War Medals. Unsure whether this was my ancestor, I tried to find a service record online, only to find that they were not available, and had to be consulted at the National Archives at Kew (**www.nationalarchives.gov.uk**).

At the archive I called up Cochrane's attestation paper which noted him as a house painter, born in Coleraine, and aged 43 years, 11 months and eight days. He was married, with his wife Elizabeth residing at '35 Borrow Street' [*sic*], off 'Manners Street' (i.e. Manor Street), Belfast – so this was indeed my ancestor. The form stated that he signed up after receiving a notice to do so, and contained his original signature, as well as a description, with Cochrane stated to be 5ft 3½in tall, with a fresh complexion, blue eyes, brown hair, weighing 117lb, and with the 'Church of England' (i.e. Church of Ireland) being his stated religion.

After his medical examination in Belfast, he was considered fit for service, and was sent to the Royal Marines Depot in Deal, England, and then to Havre, France, and later to Dunkirk. In May 1918, the record notes that he was injured on duty (although not severely) when, whilst discharging cargo on a hatch on SS *Ethel*, a piece of timber fell and hit his thigh. The report noted that he was not to blame, and that he was granted fourteen days' leave as a consequence. When he was eventually discharged from service in April 1919, his conduct was noted as 'Very Good'. He was awarded a war gratuity of £8 and given a railway pass back to Belfast from Deal.

Interesting as this was, what really made it worthwhile to travel to London to see the records was the fact that they actually included two handwritten notes by Cochrane himself, acknowledging receipt of his discharge certificate, confirming his Belfast address.

Records, 1704–1919' and 'British Royal Navy Seamen, 1899–1924', whilst on Ancestry you will find the 'UK, Royal Navy Registers of Seamen's Services, 1848 1939' and 'UK, Naval Officer and Rating Service Records, 1802–1919' collections. Several Royal Navy lists can be viewed for free also at the Internet Archive at **http://archive.org/details/nlsnavylists**.

In addition to those on the surface of the ocean, there is of course also the 'silent service'. If, as with my father, Colin Paton, your Irish ancestor served on board British submarines, the Royal Naval Submarine Museum website at **www.nmrn.org.uk/submarine-museum** contains many photographic collections, an index of submarine losses, and a history of the service from its creation in 1901, as well as several online exhibitions.

For more recent service records in the Royal Navy, for all divisions, you will need to contact the UK Ministry of Defence (p.147).

The Royal Air Force (RAF)

Many Belfast personnel also served in the RAF, including my grandfather Charles Paton who signed up to its Volunteer Reserve in December 1943, towards the end of the Second World War. He remained in its service until October 1946, before enlisting with the main RAF, in which he continued to serve until October 1950.

The Royal Air Force emerged in the First World War from the Royal Flying Corps (RFC) and the Royal Naval Air Service. Ancestry hosts the 'Great Britain, Royal Aero Club Aviators' Certificates 1910–1950' collection, which includes 110 index cards for pilots from Belfast issued with licences to fly, some of whom later joined the RFC and the Royal Navy's Fleet Air Arm. The site's RAF offerings also include its 'UK, Royal Air Force Airmen Records, 1918–1940', 'UK, Royal Air Force Muster

The author's grandfather Charles Paton (right), who ran a wireless shop in Belfast, served in the RAF from 1943 to 1950.

Roll, 1918' and 'Web: UK, Women's Royal Air Force Index, 1918–1920' collections. Findmypast holds similar datasets: 'British Royal Air Force, Airmen's Service Records, 1912–1939', 'British Royal Air Force, Officers' Service Records, 1912–1920', 'British Women's Royal Air Force Service Records, 1918–1920', 'Royal Air Force Lists, 1919–1945' and 'Royal Air Force Muster Roll, 1918'.

For a list of RAF squadron associations, and their contact details, visit **www.associations.rafinfo.org.uk/squadron.htm**, whilst RAF personnel lists for 1919, the late 1930s and most of the Second World War, are available from the National Library of Scotland at **https://archive.org/details/nlsairforcelists**. Forces War Records (**www.forces-war-records.co.uk**) hosts 'Royal Air Force Nominal Index of Airmen and Airwomen, 1918 to 1975' which may help for post-1939 research. For recent RAF service records, contact the UK Ministry of Defence (p.147).

A Roll of Honour for airmen who died whilst serving with the Fleet Air Arm can be searched at **www.fleetairarm.com/fleet-air-arm-roll-of-honour.aspx**, mainly for the Second World War and onwards. The RAF Museum at **www.rafmuseum.org.uk** has additional resources, whilst many abbreviations found in RAF service records, and some RAF slang, can be decoded using **www.lancaster-archive.com/bc_abbreviations.htm**.

The Irish Army

If your Belfast-based ancestor was instead involved in the revolutionary period from 1916 to 1923 on the side of republican forces, the Irish

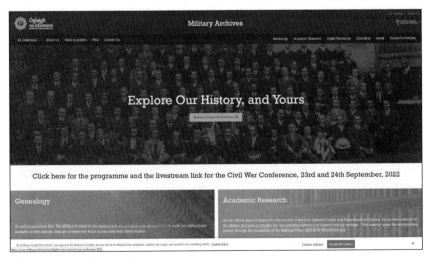

The Military Archives website.

Government's Military Archives site at **www.militaryarchives.ie** may help.

Amongst the most useful resources hosted on the site is the Military Service Pensions Collection, documenting pensions paid to members of the various organisations involved, following various acts passed by the Irish Government after Partition. A simple keyword search on the word 'Belfast' returns 220 entries. As well as *Cumann na mBan*, there are applications from members of the Irish Citizen Army, the Irish Republican Army, the Connaught Rangers, Fianna Éireann, and the post-1921 National Army in the Free State after Partition.

Case study: Elizabeth Corr was a member of the Belfast branch of *Cumann na mBan*, and awarded a small pension for her involvement in the Easter Rising in 1916. The detailed record notes her birth year and date of death, several addresses for her in Belfast on the Ormeau Road, India Street and Rossmore Avenue, the name of a sister (for whom there was a separate file), and a short account of how she was involved, including the fact that she set up a new branch of the organisation in the city's North Queen Street.

The Merchant Navy

If your ancestor served with the Merchant Navy, check the National Archives guides at **www.nationalarchives.gov.uk**.

The NAI collection 'Records of the Registrar General of Shipping and Seamen, 1860–1921' at **www.genealogy.nationalarchives.ie**, is sourced from annual returns submitted to the UK Registrar General of Shipping and Seamen, and provides detailed information on all who served on board Irish-registered ships. Of particular interest is the inclusion of the names and details of thousands of women who served on board, initially as stewardesses, and later also as laundresses, matrons, hairdressers, catering personnel and shop assistants.

The same dataset is accessible through Findmypast's 'Ireland Merchant Navy Crew Lists, 1863–1921' collection, although be aware that the column marked 'birthplace' seems to provide information on the port of registry for vessels, as opposed to the birthplace of individual sailors named. Findmypast's additional maritime databases include 'England & Wales Merchant Navy Crew Lists, 1861–1913', 'Britain, Merchant Seamen, 1835–1857', 'Britain, Merchant Seamen, 1918–1941' and 'White Star Line Officers' Books'.

The Registrar General of Shipping and Seamen was tasked with compiling lists of apprentices on merchant boats. These can be found in Ancestry's 'UK, Apprentices Indentured in Merchant Navy, 1824–1910' collection, with 103 entries for people born in Belfast. Ancestry also offers the excellent 'UK and Ireland Masters and Mates Certificates, 1850–1927' database, which includes 1,903 entries for Belfast folk, although some

Case study: My two times great-grandfather John Montgomery, born in Greencastle in 1867, initially joined the Merchant Navy, but later enlisted with the Royal Naval Reserve (RNR) in April 1899. Records from his RNR service have been sourced from the UK National Archives, which not only provide information about John's description, but also list the various vessels he served aboard, both in the Merchant Service and the Royal Navy.

His physical description noted that he was short, at 5ft ⅞in in height, with a fair complexion, blue eyes and a chest measurement of 37in. He had tattoos on both arms; on his right arm was an image of clasped hands and the words 'faith', 'hope' and 'charity', whilst on his left forearm, were three anchors.

The records then informed me that from April 1910 to April 1914 he served on a variety of named vessels based at ports including Belfast, Dublin, Waterford, and Liverpool; even on board the *Olympic*, the sister ship to the *Titanic*, for three days from 22 to 24 March 1913. Various periods of training with the RNR were also documented.

John re-enlisted with the RNR for a further five years from 26 May 1914, with this period now covering the First World War. For most of this period, from 29 August 1914 to 10 May 1918, he served on board HMS *Engadine* as a fireman, with his conduct noted as 'Very Good', and his ability as 'Satisfactory'.

HMS *Engadine* was a seaplane tender that was appropriated by the Royal Navy in 1914 for wartime service, and which was modified to carry four Short 184 seaplanes. The vessel participated in the Cuxhaven Raid of Christmas Day 1914, launching planes that dropped bombs on the German Zeppelin station there, and then at the Battle of Jutland in 1916, the largest sea battle to take place between the Royal Navy's Grand Fleet and the Imperial German Navy's High Seas Fleet. The *Engadine* was the only seaplane carrier to participate in the engagement, the first time that an aircraft carrier was used by the Royal Navy to provide reconnaissance work in a battle.

of these are multiple entries for people sitting different Board of Trade exams, to become ordinary mates, second mates, first mates, and masters of their vessels. The collection contains images of certificates, and lists of ships on which the sailors served.

The Irish Mariners Index at **www.irishmariners.ie** holds information on some 25,000 Irish mariners who worked from 1918 to 1921, as sourced from Southampton Civic Archives in England. The National Maritime Museum in Greenwich can also help, with searchable archive and library catalogues available through via **www.rmg.co.uk/national-maritime-museum**. Ancestry also hosts the museum's 'England, Dreadnought Seamen's Hospital Admissions and Discharges, 1826–1930' records, which includes details of over 900 Belfast-born seamen treated at Greenwich, and 'UK, Merchant Seamen Deaths, 1939–1953', a collection noting seamen who lost their lives in the Second World War and its aftermath. Eddie Connolly has provided transcripts of extracts from the Register of Deceased Seamen at **www.eddiesextracts.com/register/index.html** for all of Ireland (1886–1888), Belfast (1890–1891), and Northern Ireland (1910–1920, 1923–1926, 1929–1939).

Coastguards
A list of coastguards recorded in the British censuses between 1841 and 1901, including many from Belfast, can be found at **www.genuki.org.uk/big/Coastguards**. The Coastguards of Yesteryear website (**www.coastguardsofyesteryear.org**) contains many additional resources.

Postal workers
Ancestry hosts the 'British Postal Service Appointment Books, 1737–1969' collection, which contains the British Postal Museum and Archive's collection of Postmaster General minute books listing names, places and dates for postal worker appointments. Belfast is included before and after Partition. The British-based museum also offers a page of resources at **www.postalmuseum.org/discover/collections/** to help research postal family history.

Railway workers
Ancestry hosts a database of 'UK Railway Employment Records, 1833–1956', which includes records from the London, Midland and Scottish Railway Company, and various other English-based services, with over 300 Belfast residents named.

Architects

The Dictionary of Irish Architects at **www.dia.ie** details the biographies of architects, builders, and craftsmen who were born in Ireland between 1720 and 1940. As one of the largest urban areas in Ireland there is a great deal of information, not just on buildings erected in Belfast but also detailed notes on many of the architectural practices based in the city, often including substantial genealogical notes.

Artists

The 1913 guide *A Dictionary of Irish Artists*, written by Walter Strickland, is online at **www.libraryireland.com/Biography.php**.

Solicitors

If your ancestor was a solicitor, relevant records may be held by the firm concerned if still practising. Many firms have deposited their records with PRONI, such as L' Estrange & Brett in Belfast from 1670 to 1962 (D/1905). A *Solicitors Records* guide is online at **www.nidirect.gov.uk/publications/solicitors-archives**.

Teachers

The National Archives of Ireland Guide to Sources on education at **www.nationalarchives.ie/article/guide-sources-national-education** includes a 'List of Teachers Employed by the Commissioners of National Education on 31 March 1905'.

PRONI has a separate guide to the National Education Board's records at **www.nidirect.gov.uk/publications/local-history-series-information-leaflet-5-national-education-records**, detailing records held at the archive, including teachers' salary books from 1899 to 1927 (with earlier registers held at the NAI in Dublin).

A further PRONI guide to education resources is available at **www.nidirect.gov.uk/sites/default/files/publications/education-archive.pdf**.

Medical professions

There are many useful resources available online for those who worked in the medical professions.

The Royal College of Physicians of Ireland's Heritage Centre, at **www.rcpi.ie/heritage-centre**, has an online catalogue, as well as a 'Trace Your Medical Ancestors' section that offers access to a handy research guide, as well as an option to commission research.

Ancestry's 'UK & Ireland, Medical Directories, 1845–1942' collection can help to trace the career of a physician, as well as any notable publications made, as can its separate run of 'UK Medical Registers, 1859–1959'. Findmypast also hosts Irish medical directories from 1852 and 1858, and the 1913 UK Medical Register. The following is a typical example from the 1905 *Medical Directory*, concerning a physician named John Johnston Austin:

> AUSTIN, JOHN JOHNSTON, Clifton-st. Belfast – M.D., M.Ch. R.U.I. 1882; L.M.R.C.P.I. 1882 (Qu. Coll. Belf). Med. Ref.Colon. Mut. and N.Y. Assur, Cos; Mem. Brit. Med. Assoc.

TheGenealogist website (**www.thegenealogist.co.uk**) further holds Medical Registers from 1861, 1873, 1875, 1888, 1891, and 1903, as well as Medical Directories from 1848 and 1895. In addition, it hosts a '1727–1898 Roll of Army Medical Staff'.

If your ancestor was a dentist, Ancestry hosts the 'UK, Dentist Registers, 1879–1942' collection, as well as 'UK, Medical and Dental Students Registers, 1882–1937', containing a useful career summary.

For nurses, Ancestry hosts the 'UK & Ireland, Nursing Registers, 1898–1968' containing records from the Royal College of Nursing in London, and a separate 'UK & Ireland, Queen's Nursing Institute Roll of Nurses, 1891–1931'. Findmypast also offers the 'Military Nurses, 1856–1994' collection, including records from the Army Nursing Service, the Queen Alexandra's Imperial Military Nursing Service (QAIMNS), Royal Hospital Chelsea nurses, and the Scottish Women's Hospitals. The database also holds service information on nurses who served in the Second World War.

Further information on those who worked in other nursing roles can be found on the British Military Nursing site at **www.scarletfinders. co.uk**

The Churches

If your Belfast-based ancestor was a minister of the Church of Ireland, the church's main archive is the Dublin-based Representative Church Body Library (**www.ireland.anglican.org/about/rcb-library**). Amongst its many resources that can help are the *Irish Ecclesiastical Gazette* and *Church of Ireland Gazette* from 1856 to 2010, available at **https://gazette. ireland.anglican.org/archives**.

Copies of the *Irish Church Directory* from 1862 and 1913 can be accessed on the RCBL website and via Google Books. Other works that may help are *A biographical index of clergy of the Church of Ireland*, compiled by J. B. Leslie (twentieth century).

The Presbyterian Historical Society of Ireland (p.37) has various published resources that can help to locate biographical information on ministers within its denominations, including the following:

- *Fasti of the Irish Presbyterian Church 1613–1840*. An on-site database of ministers serving in Ireland from the early seventeenth century, with details on birth, education, churches served in, when retired and died, and in some cases when and who they married.
- The three-part *Fasti of the General Assembly of the Presbyterian Church in Ireland, 1840 to 1910*, by John M. Barkley. Part I covers 1840–1870, Part II focuses on 1871–1890, and Part III deals with 1891–1910.
- *Fasti of Seceder Ministers Ordained or Installed in Ireland 1746–1948*, by Desmond Bailie and Laurence Kirkpatrick

For the Roman Catholic Church, prior to 1790 Catholic priests trained in Europe, at continental colleges in Paris and Rome. Following the partial relaxation of the Penal Laws, from 1793 priests could be taught at St Patrick's College, Carlow, with a handy research guide being *Carlow College 1793–1993: The Ordained Students and the Teaching Staff of St Patrick's College, Carlow*, by J. McEvoy (1993, Carlow St Patrick's College). From 1795, they could also be taught at St Patrick's College, Maynooth, with a useful guide being *Maynooth Students and Ordinations Index, 1795–1895*, by Rev. Patrick J. Hamell (Cardinal Press Ltd, Maynooth), whilst Maynooth College's archives may also help at **http://seminary. maynoothcollege.ie/archives**.

The Irish Catholic Directory from 1836 to 1975 can be consulted at the National Library of Ireland. Some editions are also online via Google Books, with the directory from 1836/1837 available also on Findmypast. Further resources may also be at the Central Catholic Library at 74 Merrion Square Dublin (**www.catholiclibrary.ie**).

For nuns who may have joined the Sisters of Mercy, consult **https:// sistersofmercy.ie/archives**. An interesting article on the history of the Sisters of Mercy in Belfast from 1854 is available at **https://sistersofmercy. ie/2022/03/a-trip-down-memory-lane-6/**.

For Methodist ancestors, consult the Methodist Historical Society of Ireland (p.39) in Belfast.

Chapter 9

OTHER RESOURCES

In this last chapter, I will leave you with a few additional resources that can be vital additional aids for your Belfast-based research.

Newspapers

Newspapers can be an extremely handy tool for ancestral research. At their most basic, they will obviously provide news, but their greatest strength for the family historian is that they can offer a narrative backdrop against which we can place the stories of our ancestors. Newspapers inform us of the contemporary events both great and small which they must have known about, or were perhaps involved in or affected by, and at times, they may even be mentioned directly within them.

From a genealogical perspective, announcements of births, marriages and deaths can help to plug frustrating gaps in missing vital records. In some cases, our family members may have also placed thank you messages a few days after a funeral, and additional notices on the anniversaries of the passing of loved ones, in some cases for several years after the event.

Case study: When I first started my family history research over twenty years ago, one of the most useful resources to help get me started were the death notices placed in the *Belfast Telegraph* for my Belfast-born grandmother Martha Jane Elizabeth Watton Bill Graham (née. Smyth), who died in Carrickfergus in July 2001.

Over two days, some twenty-eight notices were placed, mainly from family in both Carrick and Belfast, but also overseas from Australia, allowing me to discover names of great-aunts and great-uncles, as well as more distant cousins that I had never met.

The oldest newspaper in Ireland is the *Belfast Newsletter*, which commenced publication in 1737, but there have been many titles, both local and national, documenting the city for almost 300 years. In earlier years, most titles were very much about the establishment reaching out to the establishment, but toward the latter half of the nineteenth century the chances of finding your ancestors mentioned in some capacity will increase substantially. Many newspapers had very specific target readerships; the *Northern Star*, for example, was a voice for the United Irishmen, whilst the *Belfast Weekly News*, a spin-off from the *Belfast Newsletter*, was geared toward the Orange community, with reports of lodge meetings, not just in Belfast, but across Ireland and Britain (which can be handy for pursuing the stories of relatives who crossed the water).

Libraries and archives

Whilst many titles are available online, others need to be consulted in libraries and archives, in some cases, beyond Belfast. If based in the city, a useful starting point is the Newspaper Library at Belfast Central Library (**www.librariesni.org.uk/resources/cultural-heritage/ newspaper-library**), which holds the largest collection of titles for Belfast in Northern Ireland. The site's website provides a detailed list of all

One of the many storage rooms at the Newspaper Library holding large bound volumes of titles that can be consulted in the search room (with thanks to Libraries NI).

holdings available on microfilm, not just in Belfast but across Northern Ireland. There is a caveat with the stated coverage range for each title, however, in that there may be gaps within the broad ranges cited. (PRONI has a newspaper collection on microfilm that can be consulted, with its *Newspapers Available on Microfilm* guide at **www.nidirect.gov.uk/ publications/newspapers-available-microfilm** describing its holdings.)

In addition to the microfilms at the Newspaper Library are various hard-copy holdings, although a catalogue listing for these is not available online. A list of titles has been collated in-house and can be consulted on a visit, but the library is happy for users to contact it in advance of a visit to see if a desired title is held there. A hard copy of this catalogue can be found both in the newspaper search room and on the Heritage floor of the main Central Library building (p.34).

Although there is no online listing for these hard-copy holdings, a fairly comprehensive listing of newspaper content known to have been printed in Belfast can be determined from the Dublin-based National Library of Ireland (NLI). Between the 1980s and the early part of the twenty-first century, the NLI and the British Library collaborated on the NEWSPLAN project (and its successor, NEWSPLAN 2000), to catalogue and make available on microfilm a range of titles from across the island of Ireland. The results of this cataloguing effort can now be accessed on the NLI website at **www.nli.ie/en/newspapers-catalogues- and-databases.aspx**, through the library's 'Newspaper Database', which allows you to search for titles that were published in Belfast, and indicates where you can find any surviving copies (including those held at the NLI itself).

In England, the British Library has a dedicated newspaper library base at Boston Spa, Yorkshire (**www.bl.uk/visit/reading-rooms/boston- spa**), which retains copies of many Belfast-based titles.

Online platforms

The subscription-based British Newspaper Archive (BNA) at **www. britishnewspaperarchive.co.uk** is a joint venture between the British Library (**www.bl.uk**) and the records platform Findmypast (p.47).

The content on the site can also be accessed as part of a subscription on Findmypast, but the free-to-use search screen on the British Newspaper Archive site itself is much easier to use. Many Irish and British newspapers available on the site will include stories about the city, but there are a great many titles from Belfast itself available, including the *Belfast Newsletter* and the *Belfast Telegraph*, with the content continuing to grow.

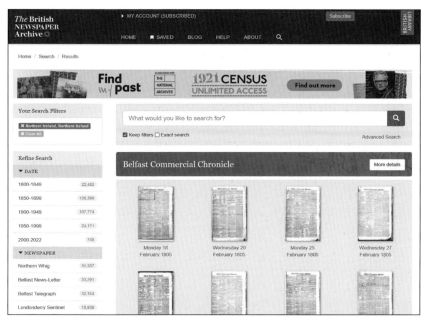

The British Newspaper Archive platform. The same records can also be accessed through Findmypast.

Also available online is the subscription-based Irish Newspaper Archives (INA) at **www.irishnewsarchive.com**, which carries some additional titles, and in some cases different coverage ranges for material on the BNA.

A digitised run of the *Belfast Newsletter* from 1738 to 1925 is also available on Ancestry as the 'Belfast, Northern Ireland, The Belfast Newsletter (Birth, Marriage and Death Notices), 1738–1925' collection. Although there is a search screen for this, Ancestry has only indexed the birth, marriage and death notices found within, which at the time of writing is for the period 1828–1907 only, although this is to be expanded.

The *Belfast Gazette* commenced publication from 7 June 1921 as the official newspaper of state for Northern Ireland, with all titles freely available at **www.thegazette.co.uk**. The paper carries a range of reports on military events, honours and promotions, the awarding of civil honours, business announcements (such as partnerships agreements and bankruptcies), land sales announcements, probate notices, parliamentary bills gaining Royal Assent, and considerably more. As well as the site's own search tools, Findmypast hosts a 'Ireland, Belfast Gazette 1922–2018' database.

Prior to Partition, the all Ireland *Dublin Gazette* did the same job, commencing its run in 1706. Just over 250 editions of this title are available via the Burney Collection (see above), with the majority sourced from 1708–1712, 1724–1725 and 1797. Further copies are available through the Newspaper Archive at **https://newspaperarchive.com/ie/ dublin/dublin/dublin-gazette/**. The largest available collection online, covering the period from 1750 to 1800, is freely available from the Irish Parliament's Oireachtas Library website at **https://opac.oireachtas.ie**. These are presented in hefty-sized PDF files of about 1GB each, covering about a year each, which can be viewed online or freely downloaded. Findmypast also offers a database providing access to this collection, entitled 'Ireland, Dublin Gazette 1750–1800'.

The following search tips may help:

i)   If newspapers are available on microfilm, but have been digitised by either the BNA or the INA, you can carry out free online searches, and note down any finds for consultation on the microfilms after.

ii) When carrying out searches for people, note the context in which you are trying to seek them. For example, a death notice may well be printed as 'Smyth, John', rather than 'John Smyth'.

iii) Try to construct searches on terms just beyond names – for example:

- "John Smyth" + "63 Mountcollyer Street"
- Smyth + "Mountcollyer Street"
- Smyth + Bell
- All of the above again with Smith instead of Smyth!

iv) Remember that there may have been more than one edition of a title produced in a single day; microfilms and digitised copies tend to feature one edition only.

v)   Newspapers that have been bound prior to being microfilmed or digitised may present problems, as pages that curve in towards the spine can be distorted when photographed. This can lead to problems when searching on databases, as the software used to create the searchable text from the image (known as 'optical character recognition', or 'OCR'), may be unable to read the article in question. Sometimes it pays to browse through a title rather than to simply rely on keyword searching.

vi) One of the more surprising finds in my family was an advert in an English newspaper, the *Sheffield Telegraph*, by my two times great-grandfather Edwin Graham on 19 September 1903: 'Address of a dealer in second hand fishing tackle wanted by E. Graham, 35 Upper Canning Street, Belfast.'

So don't assume that your family was loyal to one particular title or another – search as wide as you can across multiple titles and territories, and only narrow down if you are getting too many results.

The following table provides a rough indication of Belfast-generated newspaper holdings at six key repositories, as discerned from their available online catalogues – the Newspaper Library at Belfast Central Library, PRONI, the National Library of Ireland, the British Library at Boston Spa, Yorkshire, and the two major online platforms, the British Newspaper Archives and the Irish Newspaper Archives.

Newspaper Title	Belfast Central Library (microfilm)	PRONI (microfilm)	National Library of Ireland (catalogued)	British Library (catalogued)	British Newspaper Archive (digitised)	Irish Newspaper Archive (digitised)
Andersonstown News	1994–2005		1972–present	1994–present		
Banner of Ulster	1842–1869	1842–1869	1842–1869	1842–1869	1842–1869	
Belfast Advertiser (Belfast Weekly Advertiser)			1879–1886	1879–1886		
Belfast Advertiser and Literary Gazette	1847		1847	1847		
Belfast Citizen		1886–1887				
Belfast Commercial Chronicle	1805–1831	1813–1815	1805–1855	1805–1855	1805–1855	
Belfast Daily Post			1882	1882		
Belfast Election	1868		1868	1868		
Belfast Labour Chronicle			1904–1906	1904–1906		1904–1906
Belfast Mercury (Belfast Daily Mercury)			1851–1861	1851–1861	1851–1861	
Belfast Mercury or Freeman's Chronicle (Belfast Evening Post)		1783–1787	1783–1787	1784–1786		
Belfast Mercantile Register and Weekly Advertiser (Mercantile Journal and Statistical Register)	1840–1849		1840–1894	1840–1894	1840–1870	

Newspaper Title	Belfast Central Library (microfilm)	PRONI (microfilm)	National Library of Ireland (catalogued)	British Library (catalogued)	British Newspaper Archive (digitised)	Irish Newspaper Archive (digitised)
Belfast Morning News (Morning News, Morning News and Examiner)	1857–1892	1857–1892	1857–1892	1857–1892	1857–1882	
Belfast News			1999–present			
Belfast Newsletter (Newsletter)	1738–2009	1738–1750; 1752–1865	1738–1989,1991–1995, 2005–present	1738–present	1828–1956	1738–present
Belfast Protestant Journal	1844–1850		1844–1850	1844–1850	1844–1850	
Belfast Shipping and Commercial List	1815–1816			1808–1810		
Belfast Strike Bulletin			1919	1919		1919
Belfast Telegraph (Belfast Evening Telegraph)	1871–present		1871–present	1871–present	1871–1983	1976–present
Belfast Times (Belfast Daily Times)	1872			1872		
Belfast Weekly Mail	1852–1854		1852–1854			
Belfast Weekly News			1855, 1857–1910, 1921–1924		1857–1914	
Belfast Weekly Post			1882–1884			
Belfast Weekly Star	1889–1891					
Belfast Weekly Telegraph (Ulster Week)	1873–1949		1913–1916, 1921, 1922–1966		1873–1929	
Castlereagh Star			1994–present			
Christian Patriot	1838–1840		1838–1840			
City Advertiser	1894–1895		1894–1895			
Courier			1799			
East Belfast Post			1988–1992			
Evening Press			1870–1874			
Guardian and Constitutional Advocate	1827–1836	1827–1836	1827–1847			

Newspaper Title	Belfast Central Library (microfilm)	PRONI (microfilm)	National Library of Ireland (catalogued)	British Library (catalogued)	British Newspaper Archive (digitised)	Irish Newspaper Archive (digitised)
Ireland's Saturday Night (Ulster Saturday Night)	1891–2005		1921–2006		1894–2008	
Irish Daily Telegraph (Irish Telegraph)			1921–1952			
Irish News (Irish News and Belfast Morning News)	1891–2009		1891–present		1892–1911	
Irish Weekly (Irish Weekly and Ulster Examiner)	1896–1982		1891–1945, 1954–1982		1891–1962	
Irishman			1916–1919			
Irishman Belfast		1819–1825	1819–1825			
Lá (Nuachtán Lá Na nGael, Lá Nua)			1984–1985, 1990–2008			
Methodist Newsletter			1973–present			
Missionary Herald of the Presbyterian Church in Ireland					1855	
Monitor, and Missionary Chronicle					1853–1855	
North Belfast News			1998–2007			
North Down News			1988–1992			
North Post (North Belfast and Newtownabbey Herald)			1988–1992			
Northern Herald		1833–1836				
Northern Patriot			1895–1897			
Northern People			1981–1991			
Northern Star		1792–1797	1792–1797			
Northern Star			1870–1872			
Northern Star			1904–1908			
Northern Whig	1829–1963	1868	1824–1829, 1839–1850, 1856–1863		1832–1957	

Newspaper Title	Belfast Central Library (microfilm)	PRONI (microfilm)	National Library of Ireland (catalogued)	British Library (catalogued)	British Newspaper Archive (digitised)	Irish Newspaper Archive (digitised)
Orange Standard			1973–1975, 1987, 1993, 1994, 1997–present			
Preas an Phobail			1981–1984			
Project			1972–1989			
Red Hand Magazine			1920			1920
Reformer	1837–1840		1837–1840			
Republican News (An Phoblacht)			1972–1979			
Shan Van Vocht			1896–1899			
South Belfast News			2002–present			
South Belfast Post			1988–present			
Sunday Citizen			1973			
Sunday Life	1988–present		1988–2006, 2013–2018		1988–2005	
Sunday News			1972–1993			
Sunday People (Irish People)			1998–present			
Sunday World			1989–present			
Ulster Bulletin		1922–1925				
Ulster Conservative	1845–1846					
Ulster Echo	1897–1908				1874–1908	
Ulster Examiner (Ulster Examiner and Morning Star)			1868–1882			
Ulster General Advertiser, Herald of Business and General Information					1842–1870	
Ulster Observer	1862–1868	1862–1868				
Ulster Protestant			1961–1974			
Ulster Times	1836–1843	1836–1843	1836–1843			
Ulsterman	1852–1859	1852–1859			1852–1859	

Newspaper Title	Belfast Central Library (microfilm)	PRONI (microfilm)	National Library of Ireland (catalogued)	British Library (catalogued)	British Newspaper Archive (digitised)	Irish Newspaper Archive (digitised)
Ulster Examiner and Northern Star					1868–1881	
Ulster Football and Cycling News					1888–1896	
Unity			1942–1946			
Vindicator	1839–1848	1839–1848	1839–1848		1839–1848	
Weekly Northern Whig	1858–1940					
Weekly Observer	1868–1872		1868–1872			
Weekly Vindicator	1847–1852				1847–1852	
Witness			1906–1941		1874–1941	

The moving image

In the late nineteenth century, the print era was joined by an embryonic broadcast media, with newsreels an important resource watched eagerly at cinemas across Belfast. The British Pathé Archive (**www.britishpathe. com**) offers many free to view films, including material from the Reuters collection dating back to 1910, whilst British Movietone's collection is available at **www.aparchive.com/partner/British%20Movietone**. Many historical collections from all the newsreels providers can be freely found also on YouTube (**www.youtube.com**).

The three biggest television news providers covering Belfast were, and still are, the British Broadcasting Corporation (BBC), Ulster Television (UTV) and Raidió Teilifís Éireann (RTE). Whilst it is not possible to order up a copy of a historical television programme to view, all three broadcasters do make a great deal of historical content available to view online.

The BBC has been broadcasting in Belfast since 1924, initially through radio, and via television since 1953. The BBC Archive (**www.bbc.co.uk/ archive**) hosts a service called Rewind (**https://bbcrewind.co.uk**), which allows you to view some clips from programmes within a variety of categories. By searching with the word 'Belfast', over 11,000 items are returned, including news and documentary reports on everything from Troubles-related stories to shipbuilding items and royal visits. Dublin-based RTÉ has been broadcasting radio since 1926, and television since 1961. It also has an online archive facility at **www.rte.ie/archives/**, with almost 1,500 items available on Belfast included.

Ulster Television (UTV) was based at Havelock House from 1959 until its relocation to the City Quays in 2018. Having been purchased by the UK ITV network in 2016, its broadcast archive has unfortunately been conveyed to the Yorkshire-based ITV Archive (**www.itvarchive.com**). However, only broadcast programmes were sent over the water, with the original rushes and trims from programme content transferred to PRONI, which now holds it as the 'UTV Archive' (**www.nidirect.gov. uk/articles/utv-archive**). Much of the content has been digitised and made freely available to view at the Northern Ireland Screen Digital Film Archive (DFA) platform at **https://digitalfilmarchive.net/collection/utv-64**. At the time of writing, over 1,000 items for Belfast are available to view, with the digitisation work ongoing.

At PRONI itself there are DFA kiosks on the ground floor and in the Search Room to view the content, but material still to be digitised can also be viewed at the archive (subject to condition and copyright permissions), following the completion of a request form available on the PRONI UTV Archive website page.

DNA

The most unique genealogical record that we can use is our very own DNA. We inherit DNA from our parents, who inherited it from their parents before them, and so on. For every generation that we go back in our tree we will have distant cousins who share some of our DNA as inherited from common ancestors – the further back the connection, the less DNA we will share. By doing a DNA test and uploading the results online with an attached family tree, we can look for these relatives, some of whom may just have inherited the family Bible or the diaries our ancestors left behind.

The three main types of DNA tested for family history purposes are as follows:

i)   Y-DNA is passed from a father to his sons, and as it is through such relationships that a family surname has historically been passed on to the next generation, it can be used to do surname studies going back centuries. By its very nature, only men can be tested for Y-DNA, although women can ask a father, brother, uncle, grandfather, or male cousin to be tested on their behalf.

ii) Autosomal DNA is a type of DNA that we inherit roughly 50 per cent from each parent. From our grandparents this will then mean we will have inherited approximately 25 per cent of their DNA from each of them, and so on. This is useful to try to determine close cousins within the last five to six generations, before the shared amounts from earlier generations become too small to make meaningful matches.

iii) Mitochondrial DNA (mtDNA) is passed from a mother to her children. The mtDNA inherited by women came from their mothers, and their mothers before them, etc. Whilst it can be tested, its use in genealogy tends to be more for specialised purposes.

Several commercial companies offer DNA tests for genealogical purposes, including FamilyTreeDNA (**www.familytreedna.com**), Ancestry (**www. ancestry.co.uk/dna**), MyHeritage (**www.myheritage.com**), and 23andMe (**www.23andme.com**). Not every company will offer tests for all types of DNA though, with both MyHeritage and Ancestry, for example, only testing for autosomal DNA.

In my book *Sharing Your Family History Online* (Pen and Sword, 2021) I provide a detailed beginner's guide to using DNA for research, whilst the North of Ireland Family History Society (p.30) also runs a regular series of workshops. More detailed books on the topic include *The Family Tree Guide to DNA Testing and Genetic Genealogy* by Blaine Bettinger, and *Tracing Your Ancestors Using DNA: A Guide for Family Historians*, by Graham S. Holton, John Cleary, Michelle Leonard, Iain MacDonald and Alasdair F. MacDonald.

TIP: If you test with Ancestry, you can export your DNA results from its website and then import them into the other DNA-testing platforms. The advantage of doing this is that you will be able to massively expand the range of possible contacts that you might likely make.

FURTHER READING

(ANON). *Researching Your Ancestors in the North of Ireland: The City of Belfast*. 2020, North of Ireland Family History Society.

BARDON, Jonathan. *A Guide to Local History Sources in the Public Record Office of Northern Ireland*. 2000, The Blackstaff Press.

BELL, Robert. *The Book of Ulster Surnames*. 2003, The Blackstaff Press.

CONNOLLY, S. J. (ed.). *Oxford Companion to Irish History*. 2011, Oxford University Press

CRAWFORD, W. H. *The Domestic Linen Industry in Ulster*. 2021, Ulster Historical Foundation.

FENTON, James. *The Hamely Tongue: A Personal Record of Ulster-Scots in County Antrim*. 2014, Ullans Press.

GILLESPIE, Raymond. *Early Belfast: The Origins and Growth of an Ulster Town to 1750*. 2016, Belfast Natural History and Philosophical Society, and Ulster Historical Foundation.

GURRIN, Brian. *Pre-Census Sources for Irish Demography*. 2002, Four Courts Press; Maynooth Research Guides for Irish Local History.

KENNA, G. B. *Facts and Figures of the Belfast Pogrom 1920–1922*. 1997, Luath Press

McGEE, Frances. *The Archives of the Valuation Office of Ireland 1830–1865*. 2018, Four Courts Press; Maynooth Research Guides for Irish Local History.

MAGUIRE, William. *Belfast: A History*. 2009, Carnegie Publishing Ltd.

MAXWELL, Ian. *Tracing Your Northern Irish Ancestors*. 2010, Pen and Sword Family History

MITCHELL, Brian. *A New Genealogical Atlas of Ireland (2nd edition)*. 2002, Genealogical Publishing Co., Inc.

PATON, Chris. *Sharing Your Family History Online: A Guide for Family Historians*. 2021, Pen and Sword Family History.

PATON, Chris. *Tracing Your Irish Ancestors Through Land Records*. 2021, Pen and Sword Family History

PARKHILL, Trevor, and POLLOCK, Vivienne. *A Century of Belfast: Events, People and Places Over the Twentieth Century*. 2010, The History Press.

PRUNT, Jacinta. *Maps and Map-Making in Local History*. 2004, Four Courts Press; Maynooth Research Guides for Irish Local History.

ROULSTON, William J. *Researching Presbyterian Ancestors in Ireland*. 2020, Ulster Historical Foundation

ROULSTON, William J. *Researching Scots-Irish Ancestors: The Essential Genealogical Guide to Early Modern Ulster, 1600–1800* (2nd edition). 2018, Ulster Historical Foundation

RYAN, James G. (ed). *Irish Church Records*. 2001, Flyleaf Press

YOUNG, Robert M. *Town Book of the Corporation of Belfast*. 2008, Colourpoint Books.

WEBSITE ADDRESSES

Several website addresses were truncated in the main text using the Bitly platform (**https://bitly.com**). The following are the original URL addresses:

p.6 **https://bit.ly/BelfastFamine**
Full URL: **https://web.archive.org/web/20210802114021/https://thewild geese.irish/profiles/blogs/the-great-hunger-in-belfast**

p.9 **https://bit.ly/McMasterStreet**
Full URL:
https://web.archive.org/web/20210513124819/http://hearthni.org.uk/ projects/mcmaster-street/

p.87 **https://bit.ly/MilltownCemetery**
Full URL: **https://web.archive.org/web/20221006120505/ http://www.belfasthistoryproject.com/download/milltown-cemetery/ ?wpdmdl=111**

p.92 **https://bit.ly/Belfast1911Census**
Full URL: **https://web.archive.org/web/20190324130704/ http://belfastfamilyhistory.com/media/BelfastCensusExhibition.pdf**

p.114 **https://bit.ly/1833deedexample**
Full URL:
https://www.familysearch.org/ark:/61903/3:1:3Q9M-CSJW-G9Q1- 4?i=256&cat=185720 (please note you need to be signed in to FamilySearch for the link to work)

p.133 **https://bit.ly/SommeHospital**
Full URL: **https://www.militaryheritage.ie/wp-content/uploads/2018/03/ MHIT-Publication-Craigavon-House-Caring-for-Veterans-Throug hout-the-Decades-by-Philip-Orr.pdf**

p.149 **https://bit.ly/BritishArmy-IrishRegiments**
Full URL: **https://web.archive.org/web/20150906160221/**
http://www.military.ie/fileadmin/user_upload/images/Info_Centre/
Docs2/archives_docs/summary_information_document_on_the_
irish_regiments_of_the_british_army.pdf

INDEX